Supervision Across the Content Areas

Sally J. Zepeda
and R. Stewart Mayers

EYE ON EDUCATION
6 DEPOT WAY WEST, SUITE 106
LARCHMONT, NY 10538
(914) 833–0551
(914) 833–0761 fax
www.eyeoneducation.com

Library of Congress Cataloging-in-Publication Data

Zepeda, Sally J., 1956-
    Supervision across the content areas / Sally J. Zepeda, R. Stewart Mayers.
       p. cm.
    Includes bibliographic references.
    ISBN 1-930556-79-9
    1. School supervision--United States. 2. Curriculum planning--United States. 3. Educational accountability--United States. I. Mayers, R. Stewart, 1959- II. Title.

LB2806.4.Z47 2004
371.2'03--dc22

                              2004040468

10 9 8 7 6 5 4 3

Editorial and production services provided by
Richard H. Adin Freelance Editorial Services
52 Oakwood Blvd., Poughkeepsie, NY 12603-4112
(914-471-3566)

Also Available from EYE ON EDUCATION

The Principal as Instructional Leader:
A Handbook for Supervisors
Sally J. Zepeda

Instructional Leadership for School Improvement
Sally J. Zepeda

Instructional Supervision: Applying Tools and Concepts
Sally J. Zepeda

The Call to Teacher Leadership
Sally J. Zepeda, R. Stewart Mayers, & Brad N. Benson

Staff Development:
Practices That Promote Leadership in Learning Communities
Sally J. Zepeda

What Great Principals Do Differently:
15 Things That Matter Most
Todd Whitaker

What Great Teachers Do Differently:
14 Things That Matter Most
Todd Whitaker

101 "Answers" for New Teachers and Their Mentors:
Effective Teaching Tips for Daily Classroom Use
Annette L. Breaux

Data Analysis for Continuous School Improvement, 2/e
Victoria L. Bernhardt

Standard of Practice for Teachers: A Brief Handbook
P. Diane Frey, Mary Jane Smart, and Sue A. Walker

REAL Teachers, REAL Challenges, REAL Solutions:
25 Ways to Handle the Challenges of the Classroom Effectively
Annette L. and Elizabeth Breaux

Helping Student Graduate:
A Strategic Approach to Dropout Prevention
Jay Smink and Franklin P. Schargel

Acknowledgments

The professionals who reviewed this manuscript selflessly shared their perspectives, making this book stronger because of their insights. We are indebted to these professionals: Dr. Lea Arnau, Coordinator of Teacher Staff Development, Gwinnett County Public Schools, Lawrenceville, GA; Gregg G. Mowen, Principal, Faith Middle School, Fort Benning, GA; Jackie Thomas, Assistant Superintendent, Williamsport Area Public School, PA; and Rebecca Harrison, Principal, Caprock High School, Amarillo, TX.

The authors also acknowledge the many professionals who were willing to share their copyrighted materials for inclusion in this book. We are grateful for their generosity in granting permission to reproduce and to adapt their materials. These individuals and organizations are so acknowledged within the text.

Several people assisted us by opening their personal and professional libraries. Dr. William Wraga, Professor and Interim Head, Department of Educational Administration and Policy at the University of Georgia, made available books from his extensive curriculum library. Dr. Linda Kallam, Associate Professor of Mathematics at Southeastern Oklahoma State University, provided materials and feedback for the math chapter. Dr. Paula Allen, Associate Professor of English at Southeastern Oklahoma State University, provided materials and feedback for the language arts chapter. Beth Bean, student assistant, Department of Educational Instruction and Leadership at Southeastern Oklahoma State University, helped us in many ways to meet our deadlines.

Finally, we thank Bob Sickles, who started the conversation about *Supervision Across the Content Areas* several years ago and Richard Adin for the final layout and design of this book.

TABLE OF CONTENTS

About the Authors

Sally J. Zepeda has served as a high school teacher, director of special programs, assistant principal, and principal before entering higher education. An Associate Professor and Graduate Coordinator in the Department of Educational Administration and Policy, she teaches instructional supervision and other courses related to professional development and school improvement.

Sally has written widely about educational administration, supervision of teaching, and the leadership of the principal, and she serves as the Facilitator of the Instructional Supervision Network for the Association for Supervision and Curriculum Development. Her nine previous books are *Instructional Leadership for School Improvement; The Principal as Instructional Leader: A Handbook for Supervisors; Instructional Supervision: Applying Tools and Concepts; The Call to Teacher Leadership* (with R. Stewart Mayers and Brad Benson); *Staff Development: Practices That Promote Leadership in Learning Communities; Hands-on Leadership Tools for Principals* (with Raymond Calabrese and Gary Short); *The Reflective Supervisor: A Practical Guide for Educators* (with Raymond Calabrese); *Special Programs in Regular Schools: Historical Foundations, Standards, and Contemporary Issues* (with Michael Langenbach); and *Supervision and Staff Development in the Block* (with R. Stewart Mayers).

R. Stewart Mayers has taught middle and high school mathematics, history, and German. Stewart also served as a high school department chair. He is currently Assistant Professor in the Department of Educational Instruction and Leadership and Master of Education Program Coordinator at Southeastern Oklahoma State University in Durant, Oklahoma where he teaches supervision of teaching and public school law. His co-authored books include *Supervision and Staff Development in the Block* (with Sally J. Zepeda) and *The Call to Teacher Leadership* (with Sally J. Zepeda and Brad N. Benson).

1

The Context of Teaching, Learning, and Instructional Supervision

In this Chapter…

- ◆ Why supervision across the content areas
- ◆ Accountability and standards
- ◆ The context of teaching and learning
- ◆ Framing supervision in a context

A dominant theme in PreK–12 schools is accountability for increased student performance on standardized tests or other measures that can sort and classify classrooms and schools and, by default, teachers and their students as either meeting or not meeting adequate yearly progress (AYP). Often lost in the practice of securing increased student performance is authentic and engaged learning for both students and their teachers. On January 8, 2002, President George W. Bush signed into law the reauthorized *Elementary and Secondary Education Act of 1965* (ESEA), more widely known as the *No Child Left Behind Act of 2001* (NCLB). Since the passage of NCLB, principals have become increasingly responsible for student achievement as measured by external standards, and results on standardized test scores are now a basis for judging a principal's ability.

The challenge is clear that principals must become intimately and actively involved with assisting teachers to operationalize the instructional program . However, the principal needs now more than ever to include teachers, department chairs, lead teachers, assistant principals, central office personnel, and others in the process of improving instruction. The supervision of instruction must now take center stage as more than a strategy, as more than a way of evaluating teachers, and as more than a way to ensure compliance. Instructional supervision needs to become a habit in which administrators and all other educators continually examine instructional practices and the effects of instruction on student learning. It is as simple and complex as that.

With the increases in accountability emerging at an unprecedented rate, never before have educators and their leaders been held accountable for so very much by so very many within and beyond the confines of the school site. Given the high-stakes environment in which teachers and principals find themselves, it is imperative that principals understand instruction, teaching, learning, and the types of supervision needed to support each one of these endeavors.

Teaching, as it unfolds in classrooms, is far too complex to be minimized through a single, yearly classroom observation in which the principal makes check marks on a one-size-fits-all form in which predetermined criteria focus the observation and subsequent discussion about instruction. Teacher growth is a capital that principals need to build on and invest in if results are to be realized by students, and this is the challenge that we address in this book, because we agree with Krug's (1993) assessment:

> It is teachers who most directly fulfill a school's instructional mission. Effective school leaders need to guide and support instructional activities. In particular, they need to encourage innovative teaching, help with specific problems, and facilitate communication across classrooms—not just evaluate performance on an annual basis. (p. 241)

Krug's assessment is, in part, why *Supervision Across the Content Areas* is so very important.

There is another need for this book. Principals come to the position after serving as a classroom teacher in a particular content area or in a specific grade level; yet, once assuming the principalship, principals are expected to supervise in content areas or across grade levels that they might not be familiar. In some instances, a veteran principal might be assigned to assume a principalship in a high school after serving as principal or teacher in a middle or elementary school. In this book, we hope to fill a gap in a situation where a principal is supervising in areas in which there is lack of familiarity regardless of the reason.

This book covers in depth the supervision of four core subjects: mathematics, English/language arts, social studies, and science. However, the supervisory tools, along with the concepts presented about multiple intelligences, brain-based learning, learning styles, the characteristics of learners across grades PreK–12, and select instructional strategies (cooperative learning, Socratic Seminar, inquiry), can be applied to other content areas (foreign language, fine arts, physical education, etc.).

Principals can apply the tools and resources presented in this book to help lead schools toward improved instruction through focused supervision that aligns with content, curriculum, and instructional strategies that are appropriate for students' developmental stages. We hope that this book can serve to further the understanding of supervising teachers across various content areas and to promote thinking about the absolute need to provide collaborative opportunities in the work needed to improve student learning. Through working with teachers in their classrooms, supervisors can gain insight into the complexities of teaching and learning while developing empathy for the work teachers do on a daily basis.

The organization of this book leads the reader through the processes of supervision embedded in curriculum and instruction, key concepts about brain research, multiple intelligences, and learning styles. Also examined are the characteristics of students across grades PreK–12, and then instruction, learning, and supervision across core subjects including math, English/language arts, social studies, and science, as these areas are considered to be high-stakes areas. Topically, the book landscapes the following areas:

Chapter 1: The contexts of learning, supervision, and accountability are examined to prepare the reader for the remainder of the book.

Chapter 2: Supervision is described, including informal and formal classroom observations, the components of the clinical supervision model, and differentiated supervisory models such as peer coaching, action research, and portfolio development. Included is a sampling of data collection tools to help principals collect stable data to share with teachers during the post-observation conference.

Chapter 3: Curriculum is examined with a focus on curricular alignment and ways to audit the curriculum as a method of differentiated supervision.

Chapter 4: The constructs of differentiated instruction and instructional models such as cooperative learning, inquiry, and the Socratic Seminar are examined.

Chapter 5: Brain research, multiple intelligences, and learning styles are examined to help with understanding how and why these constructs can help to not only differentiate but also extend learning opportunities afforded to students by teachers.

Chapter 6: The characteristics of children with an emphasis on the emotional, physical, and psychological aspects are examined so that principals can better understand how and why children respond to learning.

Chapter 7: Instruction and supervision in the mathematics classroom are examined with tools and cues provided to help the principal with supervising mathematics teachers across grades PreK–12. National standards are discussed related to content, instructional strategies, and supervisory techniques to help teachers with developing their instructional expertise in mathematics.

Chapter 8: Instruction and supervision in the English/language arts classroom are examined with tools and cues provided to help the principal with supervising English/language arts teachers across grades PreK–12. National standards are discussed related to content, instructional strategies, and supervisory techniques to help teachers with developing their instructional expertise in English/language arts.

Chapter 9: Instruction and supervision in the social studies classroom are examined with tools and cues provided to help the principal with supervising social studies teachers across grades PreK–12. National standards are discussed related to content, instructional strategies, and supervisory techniques to help teachers with developing their instructional expertise in social studies.

Chapter 10: Instruction and supervision in the science classroom are examined with tools and cues provided to assist the principal with supervising science teachers across grades PreK–12. National standards are discussed related to content, instructional strategies, and supervisory techniques to help teachers with developing their instructional expertise in science.

Chapter 11: Final perspectives about the work of the principal are examined.

Each chapter includes a series of cues, called The Supervisor's Scorecard, to help the principal to apply and to practice a concept, and throughout each chapter, a series of classroom observation tools are provided with the open invitation to the principal to modify or further refine these tools.

Why Supervision Across the Content Areas

The principal needs to develop a conceptual understanding across PreK–12 of the elements of good teaching, the characteristics of students relative to their learning needs, insight into a variety of structured and unstructured approaches to supervising teachers in classrooms, and knowledge of the standards that frame instruction and its assessment. These items work in tandem and frame the work of instructional leadership that the principal must assume to lead teachers and to direct the cause toward improvement, one classroom at a time. Teachers need principals who are willing to accept the challenge of being an instructional support because

> teachers also take risks every day. There is an absurd expectation in our culture that managing a classroom is a science that people can learn in teacher training institutions when in fact it is an art that teachers master, if they ever do, through hands-on experience in the classroom. Every day when teachers enter the classroom they take risks. They risk demonstrating that they do not know how to handle every situation, that their mastery of content or methods of effective instruction are not strong, or they risk showing that they are simply human, people who sometimes get tired, or discouraged, or even angry. (Mizell, 1994)

By now, every principal is familiar with the provisions of the federal legislation, NCLB, especially the provision for highly qualified teachers. *Highly qualified* means one thing for the practice of screening applicants for eligibility for hiring and another for what credentials are necessary for teachers to teach a particular subject matter. However, what is not so clear is what it means to work toward highly qualified teaching. The principal can work toward engaging teachers in the myriad work needed, according to McBride and Skau (1995), to "help teachers become effective in evaluating their own instructional behavior" (p. 266). However, teachers need feedback, the opportunity to discuss and reflect about what they do and why, but most importantly, teachers need and want assistance. It is the premise of this book that it now falls to the principal to nurture teachers, and the first step is to develop a working knowledge of teaching, learning, and supervisory practices to help teachers assess their own practices.

Accountability and Standards

Accountability is not new, and it is not likely that accountability will lessen in the near future. For illustrative purposes, Figure 1.1 provides a very brief overview of accountability.

Figure 1.1. Milestones in the Accountability Movement

1965: *Elementary and Secondary Education Act of 1965* focuses on compensatory education.

1981: The National Commission on Excellence in Education is formed by Secretary of Education T. H. Bell.

1983: *A Nation at Risk: The Imperative for Educational Reform* is published.

1994: National Goals for Education are established (*Improving America's School Act*, reauthorization of the 1965 *Elementary and Secondary Act*), opening the door for the development of national standards and content and performance standards (high-stakes testing).

1994: Congress passes the *Educate America Act*.

2001: *Elementary and Secondary Education Act of 1965* (ESEA) is reauthorized; it is more widely known as the *No Child Left Behind Act of 2001* (NCLB).

Standards

With the focus on high-stakes performance of students and, by extension, teachers, the stakes should be equally high for the principals who supervise teachers throughout their careers. Principals must gain familiarity with several standards, and very often, embedded within the content standards are best-practice strategies. Just about every state in the union has adopted content standards; however, it is noted that standards change over time. Essentially, there are two types of standards: academic content standards and performance standards. Content standards establish expectations for student learning and often detail what students should know and be able to do if mastery of the content standards is achieved. Content standards also specify expectations or scientific assumptions about instruction. Performance standards tell educators how students demonstrate proficiency in skills and knowledge elaborated in academic content standards. Again, each state has content standards for most subject areas, and the principal is encouraged to consult the system office to get copies of these standards. Also, most state standards are available on the state department home pages.

Figure 1.2 provides contact information about representative subject area/content standards established by the organizations that support specific content areas (e.g., English, math, social studies).

Figure 1.2. Content Area Standards

Content Area Standards	Organization	Contact Information
Art	National Art Education Association (NAEA)	National Art Education Association 916 Association DriveReston, VA 20191-1590 Phone: (703) 860-8000, Fax: (703) 860-2960 http://www.naea-reston.org/ publications-list.html#standards_ for_art_education
Foreign Languages	American Council on the Teaching of Foreign Languages (ACTFL)	American Council on the Teaching of Foreign Languages 6 Executive Plaza, Yonkers, NY 10701 Phone: (914) 963-8830, Fax: (914) 963-1275 www.actfl.org
Reading	International Reading Association (IRA)	International Reading Association Headquarters Office 800 Barksdale Rd.PO Box 8139 Newark, DE 19714-8139 Phone: (302) 731-1600, Fax: (302) 731-1057 www.reading.org
Technology	International Society for Technology Education (ISTE)	International Society for Technology Education 480 Charnelton Street, Eugene, OR 97401-2626 Phone: (800) 336-5191, Fax: (541) 302-3778 www.iste.org
English/Language Arts	National Council of Teachers of English (NCTE)	National Council of Teachers of English 1111Kenyon Road, Urbana, IL 61801-1096 Phone: (800) 369-6283, Fax: (217) 328-9645 www.ncte.org
Health, Physical Education, Recreation, Dance	American Alliance for Health, Physical Education, Recreation & Dance (AAHPERD)	AAHPERD 1900 Association Drive, Reston, VA 20191-1598 Phone: (800) 213-7193 http://www.aahperd.org/

Mathematics	National Council of Teachers of Mathematics (NCTM)	NCTM Headquarters Office 06 Association Dr., Reston, VA 20191-1502 Phone: (703) 620-9840, Fax: (703) 476-2970 www.nctm.org
Music	The National Association for Music Education (MENC)	MENC Headquarters Office 1806 Robert Fulton Dr., Reston, VA 20191 Phone: (800) 336-3768, Fax: (703) 860-1531 http://www.menc.org/publication /books/standards.htm
Science	National Science Teachers Association (NSTA)	National Science Teachers Association 1840 Wilson Blvd., Arlington, VA 22201-3000 Phone: (703) 243-7100, 1-888-400-NSTA www.nsta.org
Social Studies	National Council for the Social Studies (NCSS)	National Council for the Social Studies 8555 Sixteenth Street, Suite 500 Silver Spring, Maryland 20910 Phone: (301) 588-1800, Fax: (301) 588-2049 www.ncss.org

Many other subject and content areas have national standards, including Arts Education, the Educational Theatre Association, and The National Dance Association. The busy principal should consult the curriculum in place and then explore the national standards across subject areas.

Inherent in content area standards are instructional considerations that supervisors will gain insight as they work with teachers to improve instruction. Chapters 7 through 10 provide in-depth discussion of the content standards and their implications for instruction and supervision in math, English/language arts, social studies, and science. Additionally, organizations such as the National Science Teachers Association (NSTA) and the National Middle School Association (NMSA) offer valuable information to assist supervisors in their work with teachers.

Familiarity with standards is essential, and central office curriculum coordinators, directors of staff development, and assistant and associate superintendents can be valuable resources. Curriculum guides often reflect standards, and typically during textbook adoption and other work such as curriculum alignment, instructional guides will include updates that reflect standards. Local universities, especially those that prepare prospective teachers and administrators, are another good resource to consult, as are resources available on the World Wide Web.

The Context of Teaching and Learning

Instructional supervision occurs *live* in classrooms with the teacher and students interacting with each other in addition to the content of the subject area. In Chapter 2, the reader is guided through the process of talking with teachers about instruction and given suggestions for becoming acquainted with students (see the pre-observation conference guide). Regardless of what or who is being taught, learning must be authentic and engaging, continually stretching students to think more critically and to apply what they have learned to new situations. This type of learning can only occur when teachers purposefully engage in learning to teach in this manner.

For teachers to teach in this manner, principals need to have a grasp of instruction so that they can support teachers in their efforts. For the supervisor who has been out of the classroom as a teacher, perhaps a few suggestions would be helpful, and according to Bottoms (n.d.):

- School leaders should have a working knowledge of research-based, student-centered instruction, such as the Socratic method, project-based learning, cooperative learning, research studies, integration of technology into instructional strategies, and integration of academic and career/technical studies. They need to understand the conditions that will enable teachers to use these methods.

- Leaders must be able to recognize whether teachers are using instructional strategies effectively.

- They should know how to help teachers learn new instructional methods, how to gauge the amount of time it will take for teachers to master new techniques, and how to "network" teachers as they implement new approaches.

- They need to understand the amount of time it takes to plan effectively. Good instruction requires good planning. Teachers who are expected to teach higher-level content to more students need time to devise ways to connect what they are asking students to learn with what these students have learned or experienced in the past.

- School leaders should know enough about teaching and learning to be able to identify teachers who are doing the best job of raising student achievement. Why do students learn more in these teachers' classrooms? Exemplary teachers can deliver "model" lessons and invite other teachers to observe instruction in the classroom.

- School leaders must understand the school and classroom conditions that contribute to higher expectations. They need to be able to recognize whether such a "culture" exists in a classroom and to assist teachers (through mentors or other approaches) to expect more of students.

Bottoms, G. (n.d.). what school principals need to know about curriculum and instruction.http://www.sreb.org/programs/hstw/publications/pubs/WhatSchool PrincipalsNeedtoKnow.pdf Used with permission.

Tomlinson and Allan (2000) report that "Students should be at the center of the learning process, actively involved in making sense of the world around them through the lenses we call 'the disciplines'" (p. 17). Erikson (2001) describes the role of the teachers in creating this type of environment and asserts, "Teachers who take responsibility for the design, delivery, and assessment of curriculum and instruction show greater interest and engagement with the learning process" (p. 203).

Tomlinson (2001) argues eloquently that standards and quality teaching and learning can interact in a positive way (see suggested readings at the end of this chapter). She offers nine guidelines for educators to ponder as they plan and implement instructional strategies:

Guideline 1: Reflect on the Purpose of Curriculum

Guideline 2: Plan Curriculum to Address All Facets of Learning

Guideline 3: Plan Curriculum to Help Students Make Sense of Things

Guideline 4: Organize the Curriculum so that Its Contents Are Manageable for Teachers and Students

Guideline 5: Design Instruction so that Learning Is Invitational to Students

Guideline 6: Design Instruction for Focused Action

Guideline 7: Design Instruction to Attend to Learner Variance

Guideline 8: Work for Learning Environments Typified by Safety, Respect, and Trust

Guideline 9: Teach for Success

Good teaching is all about student engagement framed in an authentic learning environment. According to Newman and Wehlage (1993), there are five core qualities that result in authentic instruction:

1. *Higher-order thinking.* Students combine facts and ideas to synthesize, generalize, explain, hypothesize, or arrive at some conclusion or interpretation. Authentic instruction introduces an element of uncertainty; outcomes are not always predictable.

2. *Depth of knowledge.* Lessons raise the central, defining ideas of a discipline. Students are asked to make clear distinctions, develop arguments, solve problems, and construct explanations. A relatively small number of topics may be addressed, but they will be treated in systematic and connected ways.

3. *Connectedness to the world beyond the classroom.* Students address real public problems or use personal experiences as a context for applying knowledge.

4. *Substantive conversation.* Student discussion involves sharing ideas and exchanges that are not scripted or controlled. The dialogue builds coherently on participants' ideas to promote improved collective understanding of a theme or topic.

5. *Social support for student achievement.* The classroom's social climate nurtures intellectual risk taking, hard work on challenging content, the assumption that all students can learn, and mutual respect among all members of the class.

As a supervisor, the teachers look to you to lead the efforts at providing sustained attention to teaching and learning. Effective teaching and supervision are interrelated. Chances are that the more principals work with teachers to support their efforts and nurture a sense of continuous improvement, the more effective teachers will become, and hopefully, the more engaged students will be. This is, at least, the optimism we offer to the reader.

Framing Supervision in a Context

For supervisors to create the conditions for learning to thrive, there must be present a respect for people, communities, and the environments in which learning occurs. To this end, "being a leader is not a property or activity but consists of a complex set of *relationships* with followers leading to a merging of mutual purpose, needs, motives, and activities" (Williams, 1998, p. 10, emphasis added). Quality teaching emerges in an atmosphere of collegiality and the professional support of instructional supervision, regardless of its form (peer coaching, action research, portfolio development) enhances learning for both students and adults.

Instructional supervision that makes a difference occurs in an environment that embraces collaboration, which, according to Dorsch (1998), "involves supplanting the traditional norms of isolation and autonomy, [by] creating opportunities for interaction among educators" (p. 2). If supervision is to be responsive to the needs of teachers, then the very structures that promote collaboration and collegiality must be in place and nurtured as teachers learn the skills inherent in these new structures. Teachers often work in isolation, as Johnson (1990) indicates:

> In the ideal world of schooling, teachers would be true colleagues working together, debating about goals and purposes, coordinating lessons, observing and critiquing each other's work, sharing successes and offering solace, with the triumphs of their collective efforts far exceeding the summed accomplishments of their solitary struggles. The real world of schools is usually depicted very differently with teachers sequestered in classrooms, encountering peers only on entering or leaving the building. Engaged in parallel piecework, they devise curricula on their own, ignoring the plans and practices of their counterparts in other classroom or grades. (p. 148)

Embed "Learning Opportunities with Others" into Everyday Work

Teachers cannot thrive in isolation. Teachers need one another for support, encouragement, and reassurance that the work accomplished in classrooms is worth the effort. Effective principals make supervision a part of the teacher's workday; they carve out time to promote peer coaching where teachers visit one another's classrooms. Moreover, principals make the time to observe their teachers and engage in discussion before and after observations, and principals look for opportunities to involve teachers in ongoing conversations about teaching. Zepeda (2004) reports there are four essential conditions to ensure successful implementation of job-embedded learning:

1. *Learning needs to be consistent with the principles of adult learning.* Learning goals are realistic; learning is relevant to the teacher; and concrete opportunities for practice of skills being learned are afforded.

2. *Teachers need to trust in the process, their colleagues, and the learners themselves.* For learning to occur on the job, teachers must be able to trust the process (e.g., peer coaching, videotape analysis), their colleagues, and themselves. Teachers need to know that feedback will be constructive, not personal.

3. *Time within the regular school day needs to be made available for learning.* Traditionally, staff development takes place after hours, usually at some remote site. Job-embedded learning requires time to be available within the context of the normal working day at the teacher's school site.

4. *Sufficient resources must be available to support learning.* Providing release time for teachers' professional development requires the cre-

ative use of human resources. In addition, outside facilitators are sometimes needed to help teachers learn new skills. Funding must be made available to meet these costs. (pp. 136–137)

Job-embedded learning opportunities are enhanced when learning occurs in the company of others and when teachers feel they are part of the organization. To support learning, principals work with teachers to maintain the momentum for learning by sustaining relationships with their teachers and supporting teachers as they develop professional relationships with other teachers.

Sustain Relationships

Building and sustaining a learning community is not possible without sustained attention to the relationships between and among people.

> We need to look at the relationships which exist between members of a school community. The formal network of connections among teachers and administrators, between students and teachers, between parents and administrators—and the informal web of relationships which exists—can have profound influences on the school. (Pejza, 1994)

Elkjaer (1999) believes that social perspectives are constructed through interaction with others, and it is through such interactions that teachers' beliefs and attitudes are shaped and reshaped within the work environment. If relationships are collegial, open, and free of punitive actions and reactions, teachers will be empowered through the process of interacting with others. In such an environment, supervisors are in a better position to develop human capital—and as a result, "we will no longer be ignoring the very people who can make a school great, or not—the teachers" (Poplin, 1992, p. 11).

Williams's (1998) message is fitting: "Professional leaders recognize the existence of indissoluble partnerships with collaborative colleagues who elect to undertake a variety of leadership roles as positive contributors in the life and work of schools as communities of learners" (p. 6). Partnerships, however, cannot be built without relationships.

Through relationships,

- ♦ support and encouragement enhance learning;
- ♦ authentic changes in practice can occur;
- ♦ safety will permeate the environment and foster risk taking;
- ♦ boundaries that typically separate and isolate people are flattened;
- ♦ teachers will feel supported as they encounter the issues that often make them feel as if they are not doing their jobs (e.g., high-stakes testing).

Recognize the Adult Learner

For supervision to be effective, principals must recognize the power of how adults learn:

> Humans do not passively encounter knowledge in the world; rather, they actively generate meanings in accordance with what they choose to pay attention to. Knowledge is thus generated by individuals in ways that are coherent, meaningful, and purposeful for the person who is creating the meaning and *in the social contexts* in which the person functions. (Benson & Hunter, 1992, p. 92, emphasis added)

The principles of constructivism are examined relative to learning environments for children in PreK–12 schools in Chapter 3; however, effective principals recognize that the adult learner can thrive in a constructivist environment as well. Lyons and Pinnell (2001) offer eight generalized principles to organize and implement constructivist-based learning for adults. These principles, which can be applied to planning professional growth opportunities for teachers, are presented in Figure 1.3.

Figure 1.3. Developing a Constructivist-Based Learning Environment for Adults

Principles of Constructivist-based Learning Activities for Adults
(Lyons & Pinnell, 2001)

Principle 1   Encourage active participation.

Principle 2   Organize small-group discussion around common concerns.

Principle 3   Introduce new concepts in context.

Principle 4   Create a safe environment.

Principle 5   Develop participants' conceptual knowledge through conversations around shared experience.

Principle 6   Provide opportunities for participants to use what they know to construct knowledge.

Principle 7   Look for shifts in teachers' understanding over time.

Principle 8   Provide additional experiences for participants who have not yet developed [the] needed conceptual understanding[s]. (pp. 4–6)

Strategies to Assist in Making Learning Authentic for the Adult Learner

Johnson and Usher (1997) report that "experience is conceived as foundational, the 'bedrock' of knowledge" (p. 1). Adults want authentic learning experiences that have immediate application in their "real worlds of teaching." Supervisors promote authentic learning through a variety of ways.

- *Ownership*. Because teachers own their learning pursuits, they are more intrinsically motivated to face the often thorny issues of teaching and self-learning.

- *Appropriateness. No two learners are the same*—this maxim also applies to adult learners. The one-size learning approaches give way to approaches that are differentiated, based on teachers' levels of experience (number of years in the school, experience with subject, and/or grade-level considerations), career stages, and developmental levels (e.g., a first-year teacher at a new site who has nine years experience elsewhere).

- *Structure*. Mechanisms are in place to support teacher choice: peer coaches, mentors, portfolio development systems, action research opportunities.

- *Collaboration*. Opportunities exist for teachers to talk about instruction and other professional issues. Collaboration is extended over time, supported by organizational structures, and grounded in a commitment to developing and nurturing professional relationships among colleagues.

- *Practice*. For teachers to learn and extend their classroom practices, they need to be able to learn by practicing and experimenting with new methods, by receiving supportive feedback, and then by refining practices as a result of insights gained.

- *Reflection*. Without reflection, supervision is ritualistic. Reflection supports teachers to "learn by actively constructing knowledge, weighing new information against their previous understandings, thinking about working through discrepancies (on their own and with others), and coming to new understanding" (O'Neil, 1998, p. 51).

Teachers as "learners" are essential as they
have been asked to assume new responsibilities and adopt new practices that are substantially different from traditional notions about what it means to be a teacher. Under these circumstances, teachers need time to be learners themselves—a truth that is rarely factored...

and is quite likely an important variable in the dismal track record of educational change efforts over the past 30 years. (Adelman, Walking Eagle, & Hargreaves, 1997, p. 2)

Instructional supervision is much more than the pre-observation conference, the extended classroom observation, and the post-observation conference, regardless of whether the "doer" of supervision is an administrator or a peer (Zepeda, 2003b). Instructional supervision is embedded in a context, that is, the school, and in that context, adult learning occurs in the company of others.

As the principal, *you* have the opportunity to become a significant other in the professional lives of the teachers who are entrusted to you for professional growth and guidance while they embark on meeting the challenges of teaching.

Suggested Readings

Darling-Hammond, L. (1997). *The right to learn: A blueprint for creating schools that work.* San Francisco, CA: Jossey-Bass.

Gardner, M. E., & Slack, P. J. F. (1995). *The constructivist leader.* New York: Teachers College Press.

Glatthorn, A. A., & Fox, L. E. (1996). *Quality teaching through professional development.* Thousand Oaks, CA: Corwin Press.

Lambert, L., Walker, D., Zimmerman, D. P., Cooper, J. E., Lambert, M. D., & Gardner, M. E., et al. (1995). *The constructivist leader.* New York: Teachers College Press.

Senge, P., Kleiner, A., Roberts, C., Ross, R., Roth, G., & Smith, B. (1999). *The dance of change: The challenges to sustaining momentum in learning organizations.* New York: Currency Doubleday.

2
Instructional Supervision

In this Chapter…

- ◆ Instructional supervision
  - • Informal and formal classroom observations
  - • Clinical supervision—three phases to get you there
- ◆ Differentiated and developmental supervision
  - • Peer coaching
  - • Action research
  - • Portfolio development
- ◆ Pulling together differentiated supervisory practices

Instructional supervision, regardless of its form, involves skills that need to be understood, used, and transferred from one model of supervision to others. Skills include processes such as the use of data collection tools and conferencing strategies. Effective supervisors pay attention to the "pulse of the school" and what is generally occurring in classrooms by "getting supervision out of the main office" (Zepeda, 2003b).

Many new principals and other supervisors freeze with the thought of observing a teacher whose subject matter they do not know or understand (e.g., physics, special education, drafting) or because they are unfamiliar with a grade level (elementary, middle, or high school). A classroom observation takes into account more than subject matter. Supervisors might not know how to talk about teaching with another professional because of myriad reasons, such as

- ◆ fear of knowing how to capture data during a fast-paced lesson in a way that makes sense for both the supervisor and the teacher;
- ◆ unfamiliarity with the processes of effective supervision because of not having been supervised as former classroom teachers;

◆ a lack of familiarity with grade levels (elementary, middle, high school), the characteristics of students at a particular level, or knowledge about a range of instructional practices that would support a curricular area. (Zepeda, 2003a)

The supervisory call is for the principal to accept the challenge to be responsive to and knowledgeable about differentiated supervisory practices that are embedded in the forms, content, and processes inherent in models such as action research, portfolio development, auditing, and peer coaching—with or without the clinical model of supervision. How the clinical processes (pre-observation, classroom observation, and post-observation conference) of instructional supervision are extended will only be limited by the imaginations of those empowered to implement and conduct supervision that is responsive to the teaching and learning needs of teachers within any given context.

This chapter examines instructional supervision, focusing primarily on the construct of differentiated and developmental supervision, baseline procedures associated with instructional supervision (pre-observation conference, extended classroom observation, and post-observation conference), and select differentiated models of instructional supervision (peer coaching, action research, and portfolio development).

Instructional Supervision

Effective instructional supervisory practices promote growth, development, interaction, fault-free problem solving, and a commitment to build capacity and resiliency in teachers. The intents of instructional supervision are *formative* and are concerned with ongoing developmental and differentiated approaches that allow teachers to learn from analyzing and reflecting on their classroom practices with the assistance of another professional (Glatthorn, 1984, 1990; Glickman, 1981, 1985, 1990). Yet, according to McGreal (1983), "All supervisory roads lead to evaluation." This is one of the complex realities of leadership in that principals need to provide formative growth opportunities that eventually lead to a summative judgment at the end of the year.

Given the press for accountability and the high-stakes environments in which PreK–12 personnel find themselves, the supervisor might be tempted to move from a formative to a summative stance while working with teachers. Our advice is to resist this shift, because teachers need time, opportunity, and support as they make sense of teaching and learning. To this end, supervision that makes a difference in the instructional lives of teachers

◆ empowers teachers to learn from examining their own practices while engaging in deep conversations about practice with others because teaching has become a "complex, dynamic, interactive activity… (not a practice that can be) prescribed or standardized" (Smylie & Conyers, 1991, p. 13);

♦ acknowledges and responds to the unique learning needs of teachers because just as all students do not learn in the same way, neither do adults (Glatthorn, 1997; Glickman, 1990);

♦ promotes ownership because the more teachers own their learning, the more invested they will be in applying the lessons learned from examining their practices;

♦ champions informed choice about the types of supervisory supports and approaches (differentiated approaches such as peer coaching, action research, and portfolio development).

Informal and Formal Supervision

The two types of classroom observations that a supervisor can make are the informal, drop-in observation and the planned, formal observation. Regardless of type, the supervisor who wants to gain entrée into the classroom needs to realize the world of teaching is not the same for the supervisor sitting in the back of the room as it is for the teacher standing in front of the classroom. Although informal observations forgo the pre-and post-observation conferences, formal classroom observations, if they are to be meaningful, must include these processes.

Informal Classroom Observations

Informal observations are one way in which supervisors get to know their teachers "instructionally" (Zepeda, 2003b). By making the time to observe the work teachers do on a daily basis *in their* classrooms, supervisors can exert informed effort and energy to assist teachers beyond formally scheduled observations. Dubbed "walk throughs" and "pop-ins," informal observations can provide powerful learning opportunities for teachers, and according to the results of Skretta and Fisher (2002), "Informal classroom observations translate to improved student achievement by using the observations as opportunities to develop a common language for instruction and to promote meaningful dialogue about instruction" (p. 4). Skretta and Fisher (2002) caution, however, that

the mere presence of administrators in classrooms is not enough to guarantee substantive instructional change. However, when administrators equip themselves with a walk-through instrument and give teachers specific, detailed instructional feedback based on a 3- to 10-minute informal snapshot of a lesson, the effect can be tremendous. (p. 4)

Although informal observations typically do not include a pre-observation conference, supervisors can strengthen their relationships with teachers by communicating *something* about what was observed during a post-observation conference. Given the need to create opportunities for professional talk about teaching, the supervisor should strive to converse with a teacher after any type of classroom observation. Figure 2.1 provides a written way to communicate with a teacher after an informal classroom observation.

Figure 2.1. Sample Informal Post-Observation Feedback Form

Teacher _____

Date _____ Time _____ Class Period _____

Subject_____

Number of students present _____

Students were	❑ working in small, cooperative groups
	❑ making a presentation
	❑ taking a test
	❑ working independently at their desks
	❑ viewing a film
	❑ other _____
Teacher was	❑ lecturing
	❑ facilitating a question-and-answer sequence
	❑ working independently with students
	❑ demonstrating a concept
	❑ introducing a new concept
	❑ reviewing for a test
	❑ coming to closure
	❑ other _____

Comments: Nancy:

♦ Students were working independently at their desks.

♦ The rearrangement of the room (desk, podium, and table) allowed you to work independently with students on their essays *and* to keep an eye on students working at their desks.

Perhaps you should hold the next freshman level meeting in your room so others can see your room arrangement. Thanks for letting me visit your room and see the work you do to help our students become better writers. I appreciate your efforts.

Marcie Stiso

Source: Zepeda (2003b). Used with permission.

Formal Classroom Observations

In a formal observation, the supervisor typically spends an extended amount of time in the classroom. Common sense indicates that extended classroom observations are needed for the observer to do more than get a snapshot of the classroom environment. Regardless of the length, a formal classroom observation needs to include a pre-observation and a post-observation conference.

Why is it necessary to include the pre-and post-observation conferences when conducting a formal classroom observation? The answer is a two-part one. First, as McGreal (1983) asserted, "The more teachers talk about teaching, the better they get at it;" it is during the pre-and post-observation conferences that teachers and supervisors have the opportunity to have focused discussions about classroom practices. Second, supervisors need to gain entrée into the world of the teacher's classroom, and entrée is not likely to be forthcoming for the supervisor who does not understand the teacher's point of view. Furthermore, this understanding can occur, in part, during the pre-and post-observation conferences.

Clinical Supervision

The clinical supervisory model comprises the pre-observation conference, an extended classroom observation, and a post-observation conference. Figure 2.2 illustrates the cyclical process of instructional supervision and the components of the clinical supervision model.

Figure 2.2. The Formative Nature of Supervision

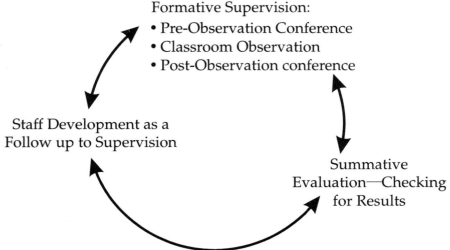

Formative Supervision:
• Pre-Observation Conference
• Classroom Observation
• Post-Observation conference

Staff Development as a
Follow up to Supervision

Summative
Evaluation—Checking
for Results

Conducting the Pre-Observation Conference

Acheson and Gall (1997) indicate that the supervisor's main responsibility is to serve as "another set of eyes," or to hold the proverbial "mirror," with which the teacher can examine more closely specific classroom behaviors. Supervisors are in a better position to "hold the mirror of practice" if they collect stable data during the observation. To collect more stable data during the classroom observation, the supervisor needs specific information prior to the observation.

The pre-observation conference serves as a means to focus for the observation. The focus provides critical information so that more informed decisions are made about what data will provide useful information for the teacher to analyze in the post-observation conference. To this end, the focus guides the supervisor in deciding what observation tool to use to collect data during the classroom observation. Ideally, the pre-observation conference should

- strengthen the professional relationship between the supervisor and the teacher;
- be held within 24 hours of the observation;
- be held in the teacher's classroom where the observation will occur;
- provide a clearly defined focus for the observation with the teacher taking the lead in identifying the focus;
- give the teacher the opportunity to talk through teaching;
- provide information about the characteristics of students and context factors such as the climate and culture within the classroom. (Zepeda, 2003b)

Most school systems have their own pre-observation conference form. The teacher might want to complete the pre-observation form prior to the conference with the supervisor; however, we suggest that the supervisor and teacher complete the classroom observation focus jointly during the conference. Essentially, the pre-observation form offered in Figure 2.3 can assist the supervisor in better understanding the teacher's classroom during the extended observation, identifying the focus, and, generally, in getting teachers to talk about their classroom practices. The more supervisors understand about the classroom environment and the teachers' instructional objectives prior to the observation, the more prepared supervisors will be to collect data that can assist teachers in understanding the dynamics of their work within their classrooms.

Figure 2.3. Pre-Observation Conference Form

Teacher _____ Date _____

Grade/Subject: _____ Observer: _____

1. The Classroom Environment

Schools are diverse. It is not likely that every math teacher who teaches Algebra I teaches it the same way. This part of the pre-observation form focuses on the *characteristics, culture, and climate* of the classroom-learning environment.

Characteristics of the Learner: What are students like? Are students on an even playing field in relation to performance, motivational levels, and abilities? Are there students with special learning needs that require modification to instruction and assessment of learning?

Culture and Climate: How would you characterize the atmosphere in the room? Probe teachers to talk about how things are run, the roles students assume in the learning process, the way students communicate with one another and you, the levels of cooperation, student attitudes, and student behavior and hot spots.

2. Learning Objectives

Content: What is to be learned? Ask the teacher to walk you through the lesson for the observation (this is sometimes called *preplanning*, an original process in the very first clinical supervisory model). Make sure that you understand what topics (subject matter) will be covered during the class you will be observing. The teacher should make clear the objectives for the class.

Process: What will instruction look and sound like? What will the teacher be doing, and what will the students be doing? Probe teachers to articulate a cause and effect between what they will be doing and what it is anticipated that the students will be doing.

What instructional strategies will be used? Ask the teacher to talk you through the method so that you understand it. Try to discover why the teacher has chosen specific instructional strategies. Probe so that you understand both the content and the instructional methods that will be used to deliver instruction.

Resources: What resources and materials will be used throughout the lesson? With the advent of technology, teachers have a variety of equipment available to enhance instruction. Technology can be used both as a resource for learning and as a way to enhance instructional methods.

3. Looking for Results

This portion of the pre-observation focuses the discussion on how the teacher will determine if objectives have been met, how the teacher monitors for learning and application of concepts being covered, and what types of assessments will be used regardless of when these assessments are administered.

Assessment: What teaching behaviors assist you in assessing whether or not students are learning? Ask the teacher to identify what the students will be able to demonstrate and what artifacts (test or quiz grades, portfolio artifact, project, essay) will be used to demonstrate mastery.

4. Focusing for the Observation

The focus is, perhaps, the most important aspect of the pre-observation conference. The focus allows the observer to

- "zoom" into the area in which the teacher wants objective data describing teaching behavior;

- collect better data because the supervisor will know what type of *observation tool* to use to collect stable data.

Source: Zepeda (2003b). Used with permission.

Perhaps the most important feature of the pre-observation conference is the focus for the upcoming classroom observation. The focus serves to

- ready the supervisor for the observation (understanding the context of the classroom—learning and social characteristics of students, classroom climate, teacher's instructional style, subject familiarity, and other unique aspects);

- ready the teacher for the observation;

- promote dialogue between the supervisor and the teacher;

- help the teacher identify a growth area. (Zepeda, 2003a)

Conducting Classroom Observations—Tracking Data

There are a variety of tools and methods of collecting classroom observation data. Throughout the chapters in this book, we offer many ways in which the supervisor can capture data during classroom observations. For the purposes of this chapter, a few ways to collect and to landscape data are offered with the open invitation to modify and to adapt these forms.

Tool 1: Focus on Questioning

The data collection tool shown in Figure 2.4 can assist with tracking the level of questions that teachers ask of students. Using Bloom's Taxonomy as a way to frame and then analyze the questions asked of students, the teacher can see the level of questioning used throughout a lecture or classroom discussion.

Figure 2.4. Data Collection Tool 1: Focus on Questioning

Date: 02/02/04   Beginning Time: 10:10   Ending Time: 10:30
Teacher: Mrs. Anna Stevens   Observer: Mr. Donald Taylor
Lesson Topic: Fractions and Decimals   Grade Level: Grade 3
Date of Post-Observation Conference: 02/03/04 (after school)

Time	Questions, Activities	Levels of Thinking*					
		1	2	3	4	5	6
10:10	How many have heard the word decimal?	T					
	What do you think decimals mean?	T					
	How do you know?	T					
	Have you ever seen a decimal?	T					
	What do you think that means?	T					
	Why the decimal? Why that period?	T					
10:15	Decimal points do what?	T					
	What makes the cents, not the dollar?	T					
	Why is .99 not a dollar?		T				
10:25	How would you write $200?	T					
	What does .00 mean?	T					
	Is that where Desmond saw a decimal point?	T					
	What instrument… temperature?	T					
	How many kinds of therm? name 2.	T					
10:30	What is she looking for?	T					
	What is a normal temperature?	T					
	Have you seen your temperature written?	T					
	Why do you think you need to use a decimal point?		T				

*Key: 1 Knowledge   2 Comprehension   3 Application
       4 Analysis   5 Synthesis   6 Evaluation

Source: Zepeda (2003b). Used with permission.

Tool 2: Focus on Wait Time

The data collection tool shown in Figure 2.5 helps teachers examine how long they wait before calling on students to answer questions. To use this method, write just the stem of each question the teacher asks. Using a watch with a second hand, measure the elapsed time from the end of the question to the call for a response.

Figure 2.5. Data Collection Tool 2: Focus on Wait Time

Date: 02/23/04   Beginning Time: 8:15   Ending Time: 9:05
Teacher: Peggy Stanford   Observer: Glenda Brown
Lesson Topic: *Rumble Fish*   Grade/Level: Grade 9, Honors English
Date of Post-Observation Conference: 02/24/04

Teacher Question	*Wait Time (in seconds)*
…in what year?…James?	2 seconds
When you think of the lessons the characters learned by the end of the book, who do you think grew up the most?	3 seconds
How does the Siamese Fighting Fish come to be symbolic of the characters in this book?	5 seconds

Source: Zepeda (2003b). Used with permission.

Tool 3: Focus on Variety of Instructional Methods

Regardless of the subject area, the grade level, or the teacher's experience, a single class period should include a variety of instructional methods. (The attention span of the average seventh-grade student is estimated at approximately 10 minutes; that of a ninth-grade student, 12 minutes.) The reader should consult Chapter 6, which details the developmental levels of the students across grades PreK–12. For each instructional strategy used, indicate the time and what the teacher and the students were doing, as shown in Figure 2.6.

Figure 2.6. Data Collection Tool 3: Variety of Instructional Methods

Date: 03/12/04   Beginning Time: 9:00   Ending Time: 10:10
Teacher: Karla Jones   Observer: Rita McCan
Lesson Topic: *Rumble Fish*   Grade/Level: English, Grade 8
Date of Post-Observation Conference: 03/15/04

Data Collection Instrument:
Variety of Instructional Methods

Time	Instructional Method	Teacher Behavior	Student Activities
9:00–9:10	Organizing lecture	Lecture, directions for small group work, break students into small groups.	Listening, taking notes, asking questions.
9:11–9:35	Cooperative learning	Assist students to get into small groups, passing out materials. Monitoring student work.	Getting into groups, selecting roles (recorder, timer). Discussing the symbol, the Siamese Fighting Fish; finding citations from the text to support ideas; presenting citations from the text to support ideas.
9:36–9:48	Large group discussion	Leading students to citations offered by groups.	Reading citations offered by other groups.
9:49–9:59	Question and answer	Ask questions.	Responds to questions (looking up citations to back up ideas).
10:00–10:10	Closure	Assignment given.	Asking questions, begin homework.

Source: Zepeda (2003b). Used with permission.

Tool 4: Focus on Tracking Transition Patterns

Transitioning from one activity to another is an important part of instruction, especially for longer class periods (regardless of the grade or subject matter). Record the instruction or activity, the transition, and the student response. (Figure 2.7)

Figure 2.7. Data Collection Tool 4: Transitions Tracking Chart

Date: 03/25/04 Beginning Time: 8:00 Ending Time: 9:00
Teacher: Mary Barker Observer: Frank Donaldson
Lesson Topic: *Rumble Fish* Grade/Level: Grade 9, English I
Date of Post-Observation Conference: 03/26/04 (4th block)

Transitions Tracking Chart Number of Students Present: *27*

Instruction/Activity	Transition	Student Response
8:00 Getting students into cooperative groups	Gives directions for small cooperative group. Stops movement to give clarifying instructions.	Students meander, finding their group members; four students ask clarifying questions during movement.
8:20 Getting students back into large group	Flicks lights on and off, asks Group 1 to send their rep to the front of the room to give a summary.	Students are moving desks, ripping paper from their notebooks.

Source: Zepeda (2003b). Used with permission.

Again, the reader is cued to consult subsequent chapters as classroom observation tools that are subject specific are offered as a means to assist instructional supervisors to collect and to landscape data collected during classroom observations.

Conducting Post-Observation Conferences

Talking about teaching is a cooperative venture, and it is the supervisor's responsibility to engage teachers in reviewing, analyzing, and reflecting on data collected during classroom observations. Hopefully, the end result of such an interaction is that the supervisors will understand the learning needs of their teachers and the supervisor and teacher will chart the next steps in the learning process.

Reflecting on data + charting teachers next PD steps

The Supervisor's Scorecard

Feedback is critical to any instructional supervisory model. Without feedback after an extended classroom observation, it is not likely that growth and development will occur or that teachers will make changes in their classroom practices. Feedback is effective because of its frequency, timing, specificity, and contextualized nature.

♦ *Frequency*—Feedback should be given frequently (this means that principals need to get supervision "out of the main office").

♦ *Timing*—Feedback should be given as soon as humanly possible after a formal or informal observation. Time fades the memory. Think of the difficulties in recreating the events of the classroom even with stable data collected during an observation.

♦ *Specificity*—With stable data, feedback should be related to specific events as they unfolded in the classroom.

♦ *Contextualized Nature*—Feedback must be given based on the contextualized nature of the classroom including variables such as the characteristics of students (see Figure 2.3 and Chapter 6), the experience level of the teacher (see Figure 2.9), and the focus of the classroom observation as elaborated in the pre-observation conference (see Figure 2.3).

The discussion during the post-observation conference should be a mutual exchange between the teacher and the supervisor.

 Post

The clinical model was worth examining because the model includes the baseline activities of all other supervisory models—the pre-observation conference, the extended classroom observation, and the post-observation conference. There are several other models of instructional supervision and two key approaches in which these models are embedded, namely, differentiated and developmental supervision. Differentiated and developmental supervision are more than mere models; these are constructs that help to guide supervisors in their approaches to working with teachers.

Differentiated and Developmental Supervision

School districts typically use the same supervision methods for all teachers regardless of whether they are beginning, midcareer, or late-career teachers. Although there is recognition that learning to teach is an ongoing process, rarely does instructional supervision position teachers in a role of authority to select supervisory options that best fit their individual needs. Figure 2.8 presents the major premises of differentiated and developmental supervision (Glatthorn, 1984; Glickman, 1981).

Figure 2.8. Differentiated and Developmental Supervision

In differentiated and Developmental Supervision,

+ Instructional practices are examined through experimentation, observing others, and discovery.

+ The type of supervision is determined by the individual based on self-perceived needs.

+ The teacher is situated as active in the experience of learning in the company of others through formulating hypothesis about practices, and developing and testing alternatives in practices.

+ Emphasis is focused on the interactions with others in constructing and reconstructing practices. Communication includes nonjudgmental feedback and open exchanges with others.

+ Adults are assumed to be capable of exerting self-directed learning.

Differentiated supervision operates on the premise that teaching is a profession and teachers should have some control over how they are supervised and evaluated. Ogden (1998) wrote

> most growth occurs when supervision and evaluation is an individualized process. There are times when structure and close support is appropriate and needed. But for those who have already proven their competence, a teacher-centered, self-directed process can elicit their best. (p. 22)

Developmental Supervision

From a developmental perspective, Glickman (1981) believes that "the goal of instructional supervision is to help teachers learn how to increase their own capacity to achieve professional learning goals for their students" (p. 3), and a supervisor's style either enhances or impedes teachers' abilities to engage in learning that is "developmentally" appropriate.

The success of developmental supervision rests on the ability of the supervisor to assess the conceptual level of the teacher or a group of teachers, and then to apply the appropriate approach of supervision with the teacher having a *voice* in the form supervision would take (e.g., clinical supervision, action research). The four supervisory behaviors (interpersonal styles) as reported by Glickman (1990) follow:

1. Directive approach
2. Nondirective approach
3. Collaborative approach
4. Nondirective approach

Figure 2.9 (see page 32) explains the four supervisory orientations and includes approximations as to when a supervisor would use each and under what conditions. The reader is reminded that there are no absolutes about which style to use under what circumstances, and Glickman (1981) asserts vigorously that "unless all teachers in a staff are remarkably homogeneous, no single approach will be effective for all" (p. 40). These orientations portray the kind of approaches a supervisor would employ based on the developmental stage of the teacher, and "effective supervision must be based on matching orientations of supervision with the needs and characteristics of teachers" (Glickman, 1981, p. 40).

It is important for a building level supervisor to reflect about what kinds of supervisory behavior would best suit the teachers in the building because the supervisor's style (directive, collaborative) will have impact on the relationship between the teacher and supervisor.

There are many approaches to differentiated and developmental supervision. When the differentiated approach to supervision was in its early stages, peer coaching was emerging as a staff development model, and Glickman's (1981) developmental approach to supervisory leadership and subsequent approaches had gained acceptance in PreK–12 schools. Differentiated approaches to supervision have since expanded to include, for example,

- ◆ peer coaching
- ◆ action research
- ◆ portfolio development

Figure 2.9. Supervisory Styles

Supervisory Style	*Audience*	*Range of Supervisory Behaviors*
Directive control approach: Supervisor directs all aspects of the supervisory process.	Beginning teachers; teachers on formal plans of improvement; teachers, regardless of experience, struggling with learning to use new but essential instructional strategies.	Inform, direct, show, lecture, and mandate.
Directive informational approach: Supervisor shares information with an emphasis on what must be achieved.	Beginning teachers; teachers struggling with learning to use new but essential instructional strategies.	Inform, lecture, generate alternatives between the teacher and supervisor.
Collaborative approach: Open, two-way problem solving; teacher and supervisor are equals searching for understanding of practice and its impact on student learning. Collaborative decision making with the teacher taking the lead in framing questions, posing solutions, and making the final decision about what course of action to take next.	Experienced teachers; teachers with expertise and refined skills.	Guide, keep the focus during discussions, link teachers with similar needs.
Nondirective approach: Self-directing; the teacher develops solutions and ongoing activities to assist with examining practices.	Master teachers.	Listen in a nonjudgmental manner; ask open-ended questions; provide clarification to questions; extend inquiry through reflection, role-playing scenarios, and dialogue.

Source: Adapted from Glickman (1981, 1990).

Peer Coaching

Peer coaching can be considered a model of staff development, a model of supervision, and a model of action research. Sullivan and Glanz (2000) write that "peer coaching is defined as teachers helping teachers reflect on and improve teaching practices and/or implement particular teaching skills needed to implement knowledge gained through faculty or curriculum development" (p. 212). Joyce and Showers (1982) provided the first model of peer coaching as a form of staff development, and they developed this model as a means for peers to coach each other while exploring instruction *in* the classroom. They believed that "like athletes, teachers will put newly learned skills to use—if they are coached" (Joyce & Showers, p. 5). The coaching model has been further developed and refined, and it includes alternate forms such as cognitive coaching (Costa & Garmston, 1994) and peer supervision (Goldsberry, 1998; Munson, 1998).

The model resembles the clinical supervisory model in that peers observe peers and conduct both pre- and-post-observation conferences, but the intents were more on coaching teachers on transferring newly learned skills from staff development learning opportunities into practice and, concurrently, into a mechanism to teach new instructional strategies to teachers. In this respect, peer coaching is a model of teaching, a model of staff development, and a model of instructional supervision (see Figure 2.10).

Figure 2.10. The Peer Coaching Model

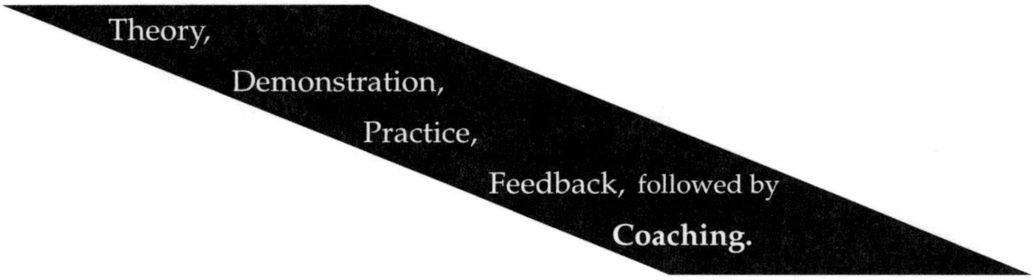

Theory, Demonstration, Practice, Feedback, followed by Coaching.

Source: Joyce & Showers (1995, p. 112).

Given the iteration of the original model, "Peer coaching either can be viewed as an individual staff development strategy or it can provide the programmatic framework for planning a comprehensive staff development program which employs multiple strategies" (Gingiss, 1993, p. 81), including classroom observations, feedback, and follow-up coaching.

Peer coaching affirms the sequential processes of the original clinical model of instructional supervision (Pajak, 1993) and includes the pre-observation conference, the extended classroom observation, and the post-observation conference. Figure 2.11 illustrates peer-coaching as a model of instructional supervision.

Figure 2.11. The Peer Coaching Model

Stage I—Pre-Observation Conference

Understanding the context in which teaching unfolds.
1. Discuss the lesson plan.
2. Select the teaching skills to be observed.
3. Decide how to collect information on the selected teaching skills.

Stage II—Classroom Observation

The coach writes an objective description of what the teacher and/or students say and/or do, focusing on what was selected in the pre-observation conference.

Stage III—Post-Observation Conference

1. Review the classroom observation data.
2. Discuss and analyze the data together:
   The coach listens, clarifies, and acts as a sounding board for the "coached."
   The teacher determines what data are most important and makes final decisions about what changes in practice will occur.
3. Plan for the future.

Administrative Support

Peer coaching will not magically occur without, in part, administrative support. Willerman, McNeely, and Koffman (1991) indicate that administrative support is needed prior to and during the implementation of peer coaching and that

> administrators should understand the peer coaching process and allow ample time for its implementation. Peer coaching does not challenge the administrator's authority, nor question his competence. Rather, it gives teachers an opportunity to improve their teaching performance while it decreases the need for administrators to spend their valuable time doing numerous classroom observations. Administrators can suggest peer coaching as a method that might be used to help teachers who feel frustrated or burned out regain feelings of control and competence. (p. 6)

Gingiss (1993, p. 82) concludes, "Principals can provide informal encouragement, formal endorsement, personal involvement, and resource designation." It makes sense that for coaching to flourish as a viable means to promote growth, principals need to allocate resources to find substitute teachers to cover classrooms so coaches can coach. Principals need to provide other resources such as materials needed by teachers to learn about instructional techniques. Perhaps the two most important resources that administrators need to provide are emotional support and encouragement for teachers to engage in peer coaching.

Action Research

Action research linked to supervision is another way to differentiate practice. Action research can extend and complement the clinical model of supervision by focusing attention more acutely on specific areas that the teacher wants to examine about his or her practice over an extended period of time. Dewey (1929) wrote, "The discovery is never made; it is always making" (p. 76), and "each day of teaching ought to enable a teacher to revise and better in some respects the objectives aimed at in previous work" (p. 74). More recently, Grady (1998) indicates "action research is reflective inquiry undertaken by educators in order to better understand the education environment and to improve practice" (p. 43).

Action research empowers teachers as the processes because they are the *doers* involved in a range of activities (testing a hypothesis, collecting and interpreting data, and talking with peers or supervisors). Moreover, action research is empowering because the teacher as doer is in a position to implement modifications in practice based on data that is relevant; the teacher implements changes based on what makes most sense in the classroom. Action research (undertaken by teachers) is research that occurs in conjunction with day-to-day classroom or school activities.

The cyclical nature of action research models as envisioned by Dick (1999) positions teachers as doers engaged in

♦ raising questions about classroom practices;

♦ developing a plan (methods for collecting data);

♦ analyzing data (with or without the assistance of others);

♦ reflecting on data and the implications for practice;

♦ experimenting with new practices.

Dick (1999) cautions that the processes of action research should not be viewed as lockstep, and his model illustrates the iterative nature of action research (Figure 2.12).

Figure 2.12. The Process of Action Research

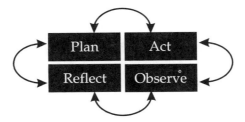

Action research connected to clinical supervision and peer coaching can provide a focal point in dealing with the messiness and complexities of reality to arrive at applicable solutions (Avery, 1990) to problems of practice in the classroom.

The supervisory role in action research can range from intensive involvement (highly directive), to involvement as an equal (collaborative), to being a resource or occasional facilitator (nondirective). Supervisors may guide the focus for investigation, they may educate participants and recipients of the research, they may assist in interpretive processes, or they may facilitate recommended action. However, if action research is to be empowering, the supervisor's role needs to gravitate to more of a nondirective stance.

What is more important for supervisors is to build an *infrastructure* for teachers to work with one another, and Pajak (1993) believes "the supervisor's task in action research is to provide teachers with information concerning both problem-solving and group process skills" (p. 257). He illuminated the developmental aspects of action research by asserting that the supervisor should gradually increase the choices of individuals and groups participating in action research to develop teachers' "thought, autonomy, and capacity for collective action" (p. 258).

Using the processes of the clinical supervision model, the principles of action research illustrate the possibilities (see Figure 2.13).

Figure 2.13. Clinical Supervision and Action Research

Clinical Supervisory Phases	Action Research Processes	Data Collection Methods
Pre-observation conference	Identification of a problem or issue	Data collection based on the observation focus
Observation	Data collection	Observer notes, audio and/or video recording
Post-observation conference	Analysis and interpretation of data; refocusing for ongoing observations (data collection); reflection on results	

Figure 2.14 offers a range of tools that can complement action research and supervision.

Figure 2.14. Tools to Extend and Complement Action Research and Supervision

Peer Classroom Observations: Peers observe one another while teaching and collect data purposefully linked to a question of practice.

Video-tape: Teachers can collect data about their own practices by utilizing video-taping. An instructional aide or colleague can video-tape the lesson. Later, the teacher can view the video-tape alone or in the company of a colleague.

Auditing: Auditing can take many forms with the teacher collecting data as an accountant would audit "the books." Data from the audit are examined and conclusions are drawn.

Portfolio Development: Teachers can track changes in practices with the artifacts serving as the data. Portfolio development as action research chronicles changes in practices and the data that caused changes to occur.

Source: Zepeda (2003a). Used with permission.

Portfolio Development

Portfolio development is another example of a differentiated approach to supervision, and the model is adaptable to fit a variety of needs of teachers across career stages (Zepeda, 1997). The use of the portfolio for and by adults has emerged in the past 10 years as a viable way to chronicle more holistically their growth and development. In an era of high-stakes accountability, teacher performance is based almost exclusively on student performance on such formalized and quantifiable measures as standardized test results.

As the era of accountability moves forward, school systems run the risk of falling into the trap of losing sight of what teachers do on a daily basis and the gains in learning for both students and teachers that cannot be measured through formal assessments. Perhaps, the portfolio is a way to examine the elusive—what teachers learn from their work.

The intents of portfolio supervision are grounded in the belief that people engage in more meaningful learning when they learn in the company of others. Portfolio supervision supports the ongoing study of the teaching process by the individual teacher alone or with collegial or supervisory support and assistance (Zepeda, 2002, 2003b).

There are numerous skills associated with developing a portfolio including data collection (artifacts to include), analysis (the meaning of the artifacts), and then reflection on the meanings in practice that the artifacts symbolize. The processes of portfolio development can be linked to supervision, staff development, and evaluation. Embedded in each process include reflection, feedback, and goal setting.

The portfolio provides the opportunity for teachers to collect artifacts over an extended period of time—an entire school year, even from year to year—and this is the strength of the portfolio. The contents of the portfolio, regardless of whether the process is tied to supervision, should relate directly to the agreed-on purposes and goals of the portfolio itself (Sanborn & Sanborn, 1994).

Zepeda and Mayers (2000) indicate that the professional teaching portfolio might include a range of topical areas in which artifacts are selected:

- *Personal* (e.g., statement of beliefs concerning teaching)
- *Curricular* (e.g., sample lesson plans and tests)
- *Classroom* (e.g., samples of student work)
- *School as a learning community* (e.g., committee work, interdisciplinary lesson artifacts)
- *Professional growth* (e.g., career goals, journals, videotapes). (p. 168)

Once parameters regarding the contents of the portfolio have been agreed on, an organized approach needs to be developed for selecting the contents of the portfolio.

Each cycle of the clinical supervision model has as its baseline the pre-observation conference, the extended classroom observation, and the post-observation conference. It was the intent of the original clinical model for more than one complete cycle of supervision to occur throughout the year. This is the lynchpin for including portfolio development as part of the clinical model of supervision, as it can be extended through portfolio development (Zepeda, 2002, 2003b).

Through overall goal setting, the teacher chooses an area to explore for the year, and under optimal conditions, all classroom observations are focused toward assisting the teacher to meet established goals. Artifact collection can become part of the data collection process used in the classroom observation. The analysis of artifacts can become part of the post-observation conference.

Based on the research of Zepeda (2002, 2003a), a model of portfolio supervision was fleshed out of the practices of teachers in an elementary school. Figure 2.15 illustrates the model and shows how portfolio development can become a part of the clinical supervisory process.

Figure 2.15. Portfolio Supervision

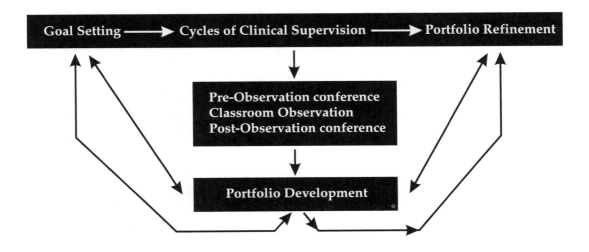

Source: Zepeda (2003b). Used with permission.

In this model, all activities—goal setting, the focus of the observation, data collection, and artifact collection, selection, and analysis—are embedded in the pre-observation conference, the classroom observation, and the post-observation conference. This model assumes that teachers and supervisors are familiar with certain skills—the skills in guiding a teacher through portfolio development are parallel (perhaps even identical) to those skills needed to conduct meaningful classroom observations and conferences.

Figure 2.16 portrays the reciprocal nature of skill application when the portfolio is used as a complement to clinical supervision. Each one of these skills works in tandem as teachers explore their practices while constructing knowledge from examining practices and the artifacts that are included within the portfolio.

Figure 2.16. Skills Inherent in Portfolio Supervision

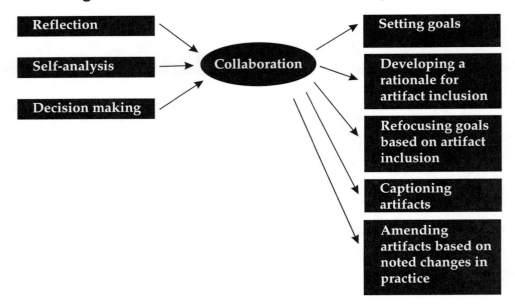

Source: Zepeda (2003b). Used with permission.

Pulling Together
Differentiated Supervisory Practices

The clinical model of instructional supervision can be extended and modified to meet the needs of teachers. With practices such as peer coaching, action research, and portfolio development, the supervisor has a variety of tools to help teachers examine their practices. Through the processes inherent in action research, peer coaching, portfolio development, the clinical model of supervision can be extended.

For example, peer coaching is an option available to differentiate instructional supervision. Most notably, peer coaching can extend the clinical model of supervision by including action research and portfolio development. Through action research, teachers develop a question or a problem of practice to investigate with data collection following. Data can be culled from a variety of sources such as instructional artifacts (e.g., lesson plans) and data collected during classroom observations.

Peer coaches can assist teachers in making sense of their practices by giving feedback from classroom observations. In the original model of peer coaching, skill transfer from staff development opportunities was a major intent. Coaches would examine lesson plans, observe classrooms, and give feedback on the application of skills in the classroom with the teacher being "coached" through more advanced applications of skills based on student responses. The interchange of student response to teacher action (teaching, for example) would be examined with the coach "keeping one eye on the teacher, and the other eye on students" responding to instruction.

Coaching keeps action research alive with data related to classroom practices and the overall results of teacher's efforts guiding further observations and coaching sessions.

Portfolio development as an extension to the coaching process can also enhance learning. In fact, action research vis-à-vis portfolio development and coaching can be bundled to form an even more powerful iteration and extension of the peer coaching model (Zepeda, 2002). A teaching portfolio can be constructed, examined, reexamined, and refined (along with practice) based on the observations of peer coaches who can, in turn, give feedback on the artifacts chosen for inclusion in the portfolio and the rationale for including items.

Suggested Readings

Downey, C. J., Steffy, B. E., English, F. W., Frase, L. E., & Poston, W. K., Jr. (2004). *The three-minute classroom walk-through: Changing school supervisory practice one teacher at a time.* Thousand Oaks, CA: Corwin Press.

Glatthorn, A. A. (1997). *Differentiated supervision* (2nd ed.). Alexandria, VA: Association for Supervision and Curriculum Development.

Gordon, S. P. (2004). *Professional development for school improvement: Empowering learning communities.* Boston: Allyn & Bacon.

Sullivan, S., & Glanz, J. (2000). *Supervision that improves teaching: Strategies and techniques.* Thousand Oaks, CA: Corwin Press.

Zepeda, S. J. (2003). *The principal as instructional leader: A handbook for supervisors.* Larchmont, NY: Eye On Education.

3

Supervising the Curriculum

In this Chapter...

♦ Defining curriculum

♦ The real curriculum, the real curriculum, and the tested curriculum

♦ Curriculum alignment

♦ Auditing curriculum and instruction

The instructional program of the school encompasses the curriculum (*what* is taught), instruction (the *how* of what is taught), and the assessment of what is taught. *Curriculum* has been defined a variety of ways. The curriculum is the content of the instructional program and serves as the foundation for such activities as textbook adoption, the assessment of student work, the instructional methods used to teach, and the overall evaluation of the curriculum related to meeting the needs of students. Although defining what is meant by curriculum is important, the definition is not as central as understanding the depth in which the curriculum spans the school and the work that teachers do with the curriculum—they shape and mold the curriculum every time they teach.

The classroom is fast-paced, and often teachers, although they make hundreds of split-second decisions about teaching, do not always have opportunity to make informed decisions based on data. This is a gap. The principal can help to solve this gap in learning for teachers through formal and informal supervision, and the principal can assist in filling this gap by nurturing a collaborative culture in which teachers work with one another through such means as peer coaching, encouraging teachers to visit each other as they teach. The purpose of such observations would be to help the teacher scan the learning environment and all that occurs during instruction. Much can be learned from observing and chronicling what both teachers and students do as instruction unfolds. There are tools that can help teachers chronicle and then absorb what occurs during teaching and learning.

Fenwick and Pierce (2001) indicate that principals report that their "most important and time-consuming responsibilities" include the work of "supervision of instruction, curriculum development, and student discipline/management" (p. 3). They also state the following:

> Exemplary principals champion their schools' instructional purpose. They are master teachers with expert knowledge of teaching strategies, curriculum content, classroom management, and child development. They regard their work more as a mission than a job. They are willing and able to assist teachers by reviewing lesson plans, offering suggestions, and demonstrating instructional techniques. They know what to look for in a classroom—active learning and engaging, purposeful teaching. More importantly, they know what to do when these ingredients are not present. (p. 8)

For the principal, knowledge about curriculum and instruction is essential, and Wolk (2003) asserts "the curriculum profoundly influences the way schools are organized and run by determining how time is allocated, how space is used, and how students and teachers are grouped" (p. 4). The principal is in a key position to provide the leadership to ensure that time, space, and resources are allocated to enhance the curriculum and the overall instructional program.

Principals and teachers feel a "tug" regarding the curriculum, because of the pressures of teaching content standards so that students can perform at higher levels on standardized tests. It is often the sentiment that what is taught is what is tested. Teaching to the test is a perennial issue that relates to the development of a school's curriculum; the instructional methods used to deliver the curriculum; and the assessment of teachers, students, and the curriculum.

As an instructional leader, the principal is in a unique situation and must be familiar with the entire instructional program across content areas and grade levels, instructional strategies used to deliver the content, and the means to assess the curriculum. More important, however, the principal needs the skills to promote and support the development, implementation, and assessment of the curriculum while promoting the use of varied instructional practices (e.g., cooperative learning, Socratic seminar, differentiated instruction) to deliver the curriculum (Chapter 4). Primarily, this chapter examines curriculum.

Defining Curriculum

There are varied definitions of curriculum, but the most often accepted definition is that "curriculum is *what* is taught to students," including "both intended and unintended information, skills, and attitudes that are communicated to students in schools" (Sowell, 1996, p. 5, emphasis in the original). According to Armstrong (2003), a school's curriculum acts as a way to make decisions based on a construct of filtering:

At one level, curriculum acts as a filtering mechanism, which allows some content to survive to be included in instructional programs and other content to be eliminated. At another level, it functions as an ordering mechanism. Finally, curriculum decisions provide some guidance about the order in which material should be introduced. The very term "curriculum" acknowledges the importance of this important sequencing function. The expression derives from an ancient Latin word meaning a "running course." Through time, the meaning evolved to imply a sequence of learning experiences or courses. (p. 4)

The Supervisor's Scorecard

The principal holds the primary responsibility to develop knowledge of the curriculum for all subjects across grade levels in the building. The *what* of the school's curriculum can be found in several sources:

♦ Curriculum Guides

♦ Textbooks

♦ Lesson Plans

♦ Course Descriptions

♦ Meeting Summaries (team, adoption committee reports)

The curriculum includes experiences bundled in a series of plans that identify specified learning experiences that can be assessed and benchmarked to see if students are learning by meeting the intended outcomes (Parkay & Hass, 2000). The curriculum includes courses often sequenced (e.g., English I, English II, English III, and English IV). Within courses are learning objectives and goals across broad areas called units. Within units the content, skills, and objectives are further defined in lesson plans. Regardless of how curriculum is bundled, there is the real curriculum, the written curriculum, and the tested curriculum.

Real Curriculum, Written Curriculum, and Tested Curriculum

English (1984) identifies three curricula that exist within every school: the real curriculum, the written curriculum, and the tested curriculum. The *real curriculum* is the taught curriculum. The *taught curriculum* is what teachers teach, and the taught curriculum can vary from teacher to teacher within any given department or grade level. For example, if more than one person is teaching English I or Algebra I, the taught curriculum will probably not be identical from one teacher to another because of varied instructional methods, teacher expertise, knowledge, and understanding of the curriculum.

The *written curriculum* is the official curriculum found in district or site curriculum handbooks. The written curriculum is typically developed at both the district and site levels, and the intent of the written curriculum is to provide teachers and students with expectations of what is to be taught and learned.

The intent of the written curriculum is to promote continuity and gains in skills and knowledge from grade to grade and from school to school. The written curriculum serves two very important purposes. The written curriculum provides teachers with a blueprint for what is to be taught, and the written curriculum identifies what students are to learn at a specific grade level or in a specific course (e.g., geometry, algebra, physics).

For the principal, it is important to ensure that teachers understand the written curriculum and that they follow the written curriculum. Think about the student who moves from one school to another within the same district. The written curriculum helps to ensure that students will find continuity in their education regardless of what school they attend in a given district. The written curriculum includes best practices concerning the growth and development of learners, the content of the various subjects, the needs of learners (more on this in the curriculum development section), and the educational goals of the community.

The written curriculum is bundled in curriculum guides. Familiarity with curriculum guides is important for teachers and administrators, because curriculum guides typically include the following important defining features:

- Overview of courses or grade level
- Overview of state and national standards
- Content specifications
- Learning goals and objectives matched to local, state, and national assessment goals
- Assessment strategies
- Pacing suggestions
- Sample lesson and unit plans
- Suggested activities for enrichment
- Instructional methods to deliver the curriculum
- Materials (textbooks, supplemental materials)
- Sample quizzes, tests, worksheets, and other materials

The principal can gain familiarity with the curriculum by consulting curriculum guides, visiting classrooms, examining lesson plans, attending grade and content areas meetings, participating in the textbook adoption process, and consulting with curriculum leaders at the site and district levels.

The Supervisor's Scorecard

Effective principals make a concerted effort to visit classrooms formally and informally to better understand curriculum and the instruction used to deliver the curriculum. Informal observations

♦ are brief and last approximately 10 to 15 minutes;

♦ can occur at the beginning, middle, or end of a period;

♦ can be made at any time during the school day.

See Figure 2.1 (in Chapter 2) for a model format to share information observed during an informal classroom observation.

The *tested curriculum* is the curriculum that is assessed through a variety of measures including standardized testing, usually mandated by the state. On a daily basis, teachers are formally and informally assessing student work. Assessments can include pen-and-paper tests such as standardized end-of-unit or semester exams and quizzes and performances in which students apply knowledge, for example, by producing a grade-level newspaper after learning how to write feature stories in a journalism class. Found within curriculum guides are assessments to help teachers to determine if students are learning. Actively monitoring the curriculum allows the principal to assess the extent to which students are learning and determine whether teachers are teaching the written curriculum. Monitoring the instructional program includes the following activities:

♦ Conducting both formal and informal classroom observations

♦ Reviewing lesson plans and discussing curriculum, instruction, and student assessment after reviewing lesson plans

♦ Participating in curriculum development work such as textbook adoption

♦ Working with teachers to interpret data from multiple measures such as in-house assessments (rubrics, portfolios, quizzes and tests) and district-wide and state assessments

♦ Providing a long-term professional development program for teachers

It is a common practice in many schools to have teachers turn in weekly lesson plans. Lesson plans, if teachers and principals use them, can provide much information about the curriculum. It does little good to supervise the curriculum by merely chronicling which teachers turn lesson plans in and which teachers do not.

Working with teachers as they plan their lessons is a type of supervision, if approached as a collaborative activity, can engage the teachers in extending the talk about what is being taught, how, and why. Think of the powerful exchanges about curriculum, instruction, and assessment that can occur if teachers are involved in sharing their instructional practices based on a specified aspect of the curriculum. A tool that can be helpful in helping teachers organize both the curriculum and instruction is a lesson-planning guide. A lesson-planning guide allows teachers to better plan what instruction will drive the content to be taught. This type of planning tool focuses on content, instructional methods and activities, transitions, monitoring strategies, assessment procedures, and closure. Figure 3.1 offers a sample format for a lesson plan.

Figure 3.1. Sample Lesson Plan Form

Teacher: _____ Date: _____

Course: _____

Objective(s): _____

State/District Objective Correlation: _____

Explanation

Introductory Activity:

Application

Learning Activities/Methods to Be Used (need at least two, preferably three):

Transition Strategies:

Monitoring Strategies:

Assessment Strategies:

Synthesis

Individual Practice:

Closure:

Lesson planning will require teachers to think more about time—the amount of instructional time; the time allotted for student learning activities; and time for assessments such as simulations, group presentations, and individual demonstrations.

The Supervisor's Scorecard

Principals can ensure that lesson plans serve as a tool to examine the curriculum by doing the following:

♦ Engaging teams of teachers who teach at the same grade level have opportunity to meet to discuss lesson planning and its relationship to the curriculum

♦ Meeting with teachers to discuss the content of lesson plans in relation to the developmental ranges of students in the classroom

♦ Aligning lesson plans to the written curriculum and refining lesson plans and the written curriculum based on assessments made by teachers

♦ Basing discussions about teaching as observed in formal and informal classroom observations on lesson plans

---

Figure 3.2 illustrates the curricula as described by English (1984). We have added a new dimension common to all three curricula, that is, instruction.

Figure 3.2. Overlapping Curricula: The Real, Written, and Tested

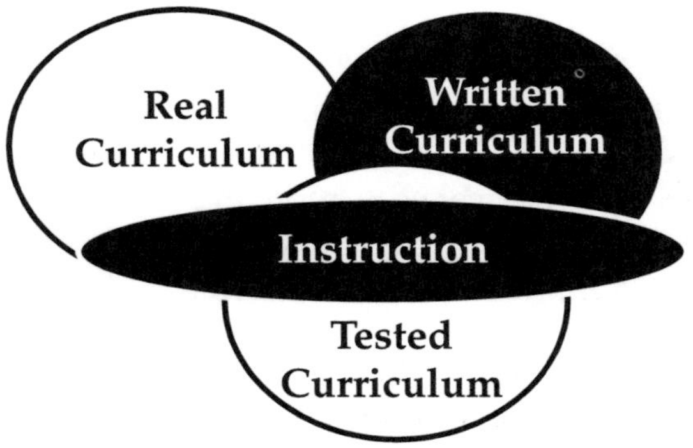

Figure 3.2 highlights the relationship among the written, real, and tested curricula. The relationship among the three curricula is iterative, and each relates to the others. Curriculum development does not occur in isolation at the school site, and often the curriculum and its development are built system-wide and include many stakeholders. Curriculum development is a participatory process, involving teachers, administrators, parents, and the community. Figure 3.3 offers a range of involvement in the curriculum development process.

Figure 3.3. Framing the Written, Real, and Tested Curricula

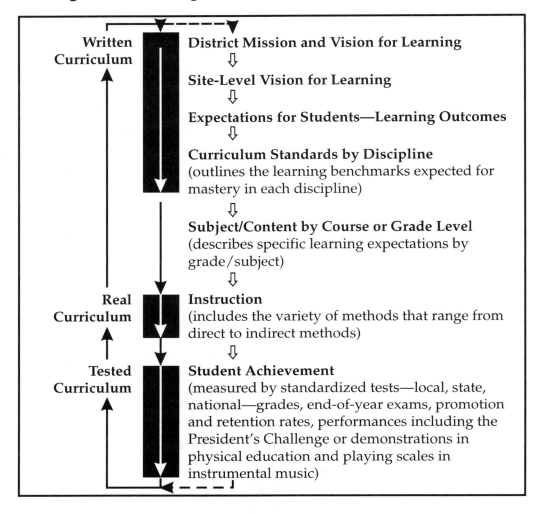

A curriculum is not static. Students constantly interact with the written curriculum and instruction. To this end, the curriculum as it unfolds in the classroom is under constant revision as teachers teach and students interact with content.

Curriculum Alignment

According to Stern (2002), curriculum alignment is about decisions and planning. Essentially, the teacher decides what is to be taught (objectives or outcomes), teaches to those objectives or outcomes, and then tests student achievement of those objectives or outcomes. The beginnings of curriculum alignment were wed to the emergence of the accountability movement in hope of creating more effective schools (March & Willis, 2003) by creating mechanisms to assess local and state goals against student performance on standardized tests. Henson (1995) credits English with the purpose of curriculum alignment: "Curriculum alignment means adjusting the planned curriculum so that the taught curriculum will parallel the tested curriculum" (p. 190). Broadly, curriculum alignment ensures a planned relationship among the written, the taught, and the tested curricula. The criticism often made is that curriculum alignment supports teaching to the test because the curriculum alignment process begins with examining goals to see how they are aligned and met through the results of the testing program. Another process involved with curriculum alignment is to assess instruction related to the standards (e.g., content).

The Supervisor's Scorecard

Principals ensure that teachers new to the building regardless of their experience level understand the written curriculum. Strategies include

♦ enlisting the support of mentor or master teachers in reviewing the curriculum with newcomers;

♦ providing release time for new teachers to work with district-level curriculum coordinators;

♦ reviewing and giving immediate feedback to lesson plans and informal and formal classroom observations.

There are three steps involved in curriculum alignment that center on skills, according to McNeil (1990):

1. The essential skills to be taught are defined and the list of skills are distributed to teachers.

2. Test items for the essential skills are developed with test items retaining the same format as those found in the textbook so that the *skill* is being measured.

3. Teachers must be certain to focus their teaching on the desired skills. (p. 210, emphasis in the original)

By going through these steps, McNeil (1990) believed that school systems could achieve a vertical and horizontal alignment of the curriculum to assure that similar content and skills were addressed at each subject area and content level throughout systems. It was the hope that efforts at curriculum alignment would provide a focus for the instructional program by steering teachers and students to what were the most essential skills to be mastered and knowledge to be learned.

Key Concepts

Horizontal Alignment: Content aligns within a grade or a course from one teacher to another.

Vertical Alignment: Content aligns from one grade level to others above (middle school, high school) and below (elementary school and middle school).

Vertical articulation, according to DeMott (1999) is a process that requires

1. finding the leaders at the different levels;

2 creating and supporting an articulation committee;

3. determining what should be articulated;

4. drafting a scope and sequence paper;

5. reviewing and comparing the exit objectives and competencies;

6. adopting courses and adapting programs to ensure success;

7. reviewing, revising, and updating the articulation agreement to keep it current. (pp. 22–24)

Figure 3.4 depicts a highly aligned school curriculum. The alignment of the real, written, and tested curricula is found in the overlapping areas; the larger this area, the more aligned a school's overall curriculum is.

Figure 3.4. A Highly Aligned Curriculum

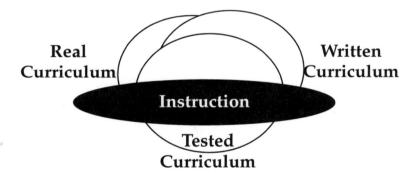

The area of alignment as depicted in Figure 3.4 is perhaps most worth examining. In most districts, there exists a scope and sequence: Teachers spend countless hours developing the written curriculum and constructing curriculum guides. The process in which teachers are most often involved is during the time immediately before and then after a textbook adoption process. As textbooks are being selected, learning objectives and goals (both local and state) are examined. During this examination process, teachers

♦ modify goals and objectives based on recency of local, state, and national standards (or perhaps by the professional organizations that develop these standards such as the National Council of Teachers of Mathematics);

♦ select textbooks and other resources necessary to meet content goals based on standards;

♦ refine district curriculum guides to align with goals and objectives;

♦ rethink methods to assess student mastery.

When these tasks (and perhaps others) have been completed, the written curriculum is in place.

The taught curriculum develops because of what teachers do in their classrooms, making subtle changes to adapt the written curriculum to the needs of students within the context of the classroom. From a practice perspective, there is a critical area linking the real, written, and tested curricula—instructional strategies used to deliver the curricula. Differentiating and varying instructional strategies bring life to the curriculum (Chapter 4). The impact and effectiveness of the real and written curricula, coupled with the impact of instruction, are measured within the sphere of the tested curriculum. The tested curriculum occurs at multiple stages:

♦ Daily assessment associated with teaching (live interaction)

♦ Teacher-driven formal assessments such as daily quizzes, chapter/unit tests, midterm/final examinations, and presentation of portfolios, a mock trial, a reenactment of a major historical event

♦ Performance on state mandated tests

However, what the building level does to align its curriculum must always lead back to what has been established at the district level which should reflect state and national standards for student achievement (see Figure 3.3).

The principal's work is to ensure that site level efforts enact policy. The curriculum adopted by the board of education is policy, and by aligning the work teachers do to assess their efforts in reaching the goals of curriculum helps to ensure that policy is enacted. In the end, the principal needs to be able to give feedback to help teachers learn from their efforts to bring the curriculum to life in the classroom. Teachers want feedback that helps them realize the changes needed in practice to move closer to the mark of achieving curricular goals and to enhance student learning.

The Supervisor's Scorecard

A curriculum is coordinated when the principles are articulated from grade-to-grade from preschool all the way to postsecondary and backward. The principal provides leadership by continually assessing these areas:

♦ Enrichment and remediation opportunities

♦ Interdisciplinary connections between content and grade levels

♦ Student performance (grades, testing results on local, state, and national exams, and end-of-course tests)

In addition to feedback, teachers need another resource that only the principal can provide—time during the day to have the opportunity to work with curricular issues such as the scope and sequence of the curriculum that ensures alignment. Teachers need the opportunity to work with the teachers who teach the same subjects at grade level and beyond grade level to ensure "in-site" (in-house), "trans-site" (across sites within a system), and overall alignment. The principal can enhance the work of teachers in the process of aligning the curriculum by

♦ involving teachers from the beginning of the process;

♦ enlisting outside experts to evaluate existing curriculum and delivery systems;

♦ using more than one method of evaluation;

♦ making necessary adjustments within the process to increase or maintain teacher "buy-in";

♦ being very clear about the final product before mapping details or identifying skills;

♦ making every effort to involve each grade level in the process;

♦ including counselors, itinerant teachers, and paraprofessionals in the process whenever possible;

♦ being goal oriented, but leaving enough time during the process for reflection, related staff development, and self-study (or group study).

Curriculum alignment begins at the district level with the development of the PreK–12 curriculum (complete with a scope and sequence of knowledge and skills in each content area along with district and state content standards and assessments). Alignment, however, is not likely without a systematic approach in which classroom assessments (quiz and test results, end-of-course exams) are linked to state and national tests. To make this connection, teachers must be involved in the process of revisiting their work, and to do this, teachers need the support of the principal.

Specific supports would include professional development tailored to assist teachers in acquiring the skills, training, tools, and resources needed to implement a scope and sequence that prepares students to meet the standards in which they will be assessed as delineated in district-level curriculum guides.

Auditing Curriculum and Instruction

Teachers learn more about their teaching and its impact on students through systemic examination of currently used instructional practices. With the whirlwind of raising the accountability bar, often teachers feel the pressure to try new strategies as a means to achieve goals and objectives embedded in standards. Before abandoning old strategies for new classroom strategies, it is important for the principal to provide opportunities for teachers to inventory currently used instructional strategies. Through such examination, modifications can be made based on objective data from classroom observations and artifacts such as lesson plans that can then be examined against results on assessments such as standardized tests, student-generated artifacts such as portfolios, and teacher-generated measures such as tests and quizzes.

One way teachers can examine their practices to make informed judgments about their teaching and its relationship to curriculum, instruction, and student learning is to conduct formal audits. The following strategies can be helpful in assisting the principal in leading teachers through the process of auditing their instructional practices.

Audits

Audits are data collection tools from which teachers are able to make informed decisions based on data concerning the curriculum and instructional practices. In addition, based on information gathered through audits, the principal can work with teachers to identify staff development needs, potential focus areas for classroom observations, and questions for further action research. Figure 3.5 depicts the relationship among curricular audits, staff development, and supervision.

Three types of audits (curriculum mapping, content pacing, and instructional pacing) are discussed in the next sections, against the backdrop of instructional practices as a way to assist principals with working with teachers and the instructional program.

Figure 3.5. Auditing the Instructional Program

Auditing
Auditing is the process of examining, through the systematic collection of data, exactly how the school's curriculum is being delivered. Auditing can be conducted with a supervisory focus, as a part of a staff development initiative, or through action research.

Curriculum Maps	Content Pacing	Instructional Pacing
Track the content and objectives covered	Tracks time spent on given unit and/or specific objective(s)	Tracks time spent on specific instruction and classroom activities

Action Research
Data collected are analyzed to answer question(s) identified through supervisory practice, staff development or action research.

Staff development needs identified	Focus identified for future supervisory action	Questions for action research identified

Curriculum Mapping

Curriculum mapping is a method of depicting pictorially the real curriculum. Curriculum maps can be designed to represent a multiyear sequence of courses (e.g., English I, English II, English III, and English IV), show a specific course over a year or semester, or focus on a single class period. It is important to remember that curriculum mapping is a tool for *program* evaluation, not *teacher* evaluation. However, a supervisor or peer coach could assist a teacher to map his or her class period by notating items such as instructional strategies used and their duration. By working with another individual, the teacher would not become burdened with tracking information while teaching. The purpose of curriculum mapping is to determine what is being taught, how it is being taught, and the amount of class time expended to teach it.

The following curriculum map depicts a high school social studies course on a block schedule format for one week. For illustrative purposes, the map provides data about the topic (curriculum), instructional strategies used to teach concepts, and the amount of time spent on each topic (see Figure 3.6). This map could be landscaped differently to show more elaboration on the curriculum without noting the instructional strategies and the time spent on each strategy. The principal is encouraged to modify this map to landscape data that will help teachers "telescope" on a specific aspect of the curriculum, the strategies used to teach the curriculum, and the time afforded to each activity.

Figure 3.6. Sample Weekly Curriculum Map

	Topic Taught	Strategies Used	Duration	Cumulative Time Totals
Monday Jan 11	Causes of World War I People and Places of World War I	*Lecture:* How it started *Pairs:* Arrange list of events in chronological order *Groups:* Worksheet/map, World War I	15 min. 15 min. 25 min.	L = 15 C = 40
Tuesday Jan 12	Central Powers Triple Alliance Triple Entente	*Lecture:* Which country goes where? *Groups:* Mock war planning conference *Discussion:* Politics and World War I	10 min. 35 min. 10 min.	L = 25 C = 75 D = 10
Wednesday Jan 13	Battle of the Marne and the Battle of Verdun	*Lecture:* Setting the scene *Simulation:* Battle Planning Conference *Discussion:* What would you have done Differently?	10 min. 30 min. 15 min.	L = 35 C = 75 D = 25 S = 30
Thursday Jan 14	Russian Revolution and American Entry into World War I	*Lecture:* Connecting the Two Events *Groups:* Worksheets on Russian Revolution*Discussion:* Was America obliged to enter World War I?	10 min. 15 min. 30 min.	L = 45 C = 90 D = 55 S = 30
Friday Jan 15	The Treaty of Versailles	*Lecture:* Setting the Stage *Simulation:* Reenactment of the Versailles Peace Conference *Discussion:* Wrap-up	5 min. 40 min. 10 min.	L = 50 C = 90 D = 65 S = 70

Legend: L = Lecture; C = Cooperative Learning; D = Discussion; S = Simulations

By analyzing the data collected through the mapping process, teachers can become more informed about what they teach, how they teach it, and then make informed adjustments in instructional pacing. When teachers map their teaching, the aggregation of data composes a solid foundation for planning further staff development and pinpointing specific ways the principal or peer coaches can be of assistance. Effective principals empower teachers by valuing their voices in making data-driven decisions concerning what staff development is needed to assist in refining instructional skills and developing deeper knowledge and awareness about the curriculum. Principals can support open-ended and ongoing discussions by encouraging teachers to

- discuss their findings with colleagues across subject levels;
- identify commonalties;
- then assist with providing staff development based on these findings.

Instructional Pacing

The refinement of teaching strategies creates the need for teachers to be able to pace instruction. Many variables affect the pacing of instruction:

- The experience of the teacher (beginning teacher; veteran teacher teaching in a new area)
- Standards (some content standards might be new to teachers)
- The range of student ability levels in the classroom
- Prior student knowledge

Flexibility in pacing is desirable; however, teachers need to plan how long to spend on a concept, how long each learning activity should last, and how the transitions from one activity to the next will occur. Pacing is also important for teachers to answer certain fundamental questions, for example, "Have students had enough time to learn and apply knowledge?" Pacing can assist teachers in determining how much time they spend on a particular component of the curriculum. This information is important when assessing whether students have gained mastery over the content. Think of the powerful lessons teachers can learn if they are tracking their instruction relative to time and then simultaneously examining data such as a final essay, the results of a quiz, or subscores on standardized tests.

Figure 3.7 depicts a single class period with approximate times for each activity.

Figure 3.7. Sample Instructional Pacing Guide: Geometry

Teacher: Jones   Course: Geometry   Date: January 13, 2004

Objective(s): Classification of Triangles and their Properties

State/District Objective Correlation: IIa, b, d

Classroom Events	*Anticipated Time Needed*
Explanation	
Introductory Activity: Discussion of practical applications of triangles in areas such as surveying, construction, and sports.	10 minutes
Application	
Learning Activities/Methodologies	20 minutes
1. Cooperative Learning: students will construct triangles according to instructions on chalkboard, using pencil, straight-edge, and compass.	15 minutes
	5 minutes
2. Cooperative Learning/Inquiry: students will use protractor and ruler measure all angles and sides within each triangle.	5 minutes
Transition Strategies	
1. Teacher-led discussion to determine what characteristics should be used to classify triangles and to introduce needed terminology.	7 minutes
2. Teacher will solicit group input concerning patterns discovered during Learning Activity #2	5 minutes
Monitoring Strategies	
Teacher will monitor student learning through questioning and monitoring by walking around.	
Assessment Strategies	
Student constructions will be placed in portfolios.	3 minutes
Closure	
Discuss how right angles may be used to construct a baseball field and how those right angles are related to tomorrow's topic: the square.	7 minutes
Total Time Used	77 minutes

Instructional supervision (administratively or peer driven) can be enhanced by using content and instructional pacing techniques. With the teacher and supervisor (or peer coach) collecting data about content pacing and instructional strategies, decisions that are more informed can be made regarding pacing, content coverage, and student outcomes.

Suggested Readings

Armstrong, D. G. (2003). *Curriculum today.* Upper Saddle River, NJ: Merrill Prentice Hall.

Ellis, A. K. (2004). *Exemplars of curriculum theory.* Larchmont, NY: Eye On Education

Erickson, L. (2001). *Stirring the head, heart, and soul: Redefining curriculum and instruction.* Thousand Oaks, CA: Corwin Press.

4

Linkages Among Curriculum, Learning, and Instruction

In this Chapter...

♦ Linkages to learning
- Teacher-centered paradigm
- Student-directed learning and constructivism
- Differentiating instruction
♦ Instructional methods
- Socratic Seminars
- Cooperative Learning
- Simulations
- Inquiry
♦ Enhancing instructional methods
♦ Differentiated assessment

Instruction drives the curriculum, and teachers bring life to the curriculum through the instructional strategies they use. The foundation of a school is its teachers, and they must be ready to support and complement learning. However, learning can only be transformed when teaching is transformed first, as Darling-Hammond (1995) indicates:

> The importance of transforming teaching is becoming ever clearer as schools are expected to find ways to support and connect with the needs of all learners... teachers must be able to develop learning experiences that accommodate a variety of cognitive styles, with activities that broaden rather than reduce the range of possibilities for learning. (p. 155)

Teaching is iterative, and teachers continually adjust teaching strategies based on the interactions they have with learners. Teacher engagement in the learning process is critical, and Erikson (2001) asserts, "Teachers who take responsibility for the design, delivery, and assessment of curriculum and instruction show greater interest and engagement with the learning process" (p. 203).

Effective principals have a mastery of various instructional methods and models that encourage student achievement, and although there are several instructional methods that have been researched for their overall effects on student learning, there is no magic formula for what works best for all students in any given classroom. What we do know, however, is that teaching can only be transformative when students learn. This chapter explores the overall construct of learning and a few instructional methods that can assist the principal working with teachers interested in offering alternatives to the teacher-centered paradigm, often referred to as the "Sage on the Stage Syndrome," are examined.

Linkages to Learning

Chapter 6 provides great detail on the characteristics of learners across the PreK–12 spectrum, and the principal is encouraged to reflect on the characteristics of learners and to draw linkages to how these characteristics should shape instruction. Chapter 5 examines learning relative to multiple intelligences, brain research, and learning styles. Both Chapters 5 and 6 should be consulted as sources to enhance understanding about learning and its relationship to instruction.

Regardless of what strategy is used to teach, instruction must be differentiated to meet the individual and collective needs of students. Some students come to school better prepared to learn than others; some students have more innate talents than others; some students understand the language better than others; and some students have learning disabilities—all of which require teachers to modify instruction, tailoring learning to ensure higher levels of success.

The Teacher-Centered Paradigm

Jensen (1998) identifies three models of the teacher-centered paradigm: apprenticeship, conveyor belt, and behaviorism (pp. 1–2). In the *apprenticeship* model, the education process was embedded in the business community. To learn a trade, one sought the advice and mentorship of someone practicing that trade. The influence of the system crossed the boundaries of social class and economic status.

In the *conveyor belt* model, ushered in by the Industrial Revolution, education assumed a distinct identity for the first time. Students were gathered together in one place for learning. The curriculum became standardized: Everyone studied literature, mathematics, and history, for example. The conveyor belt model emphasized the importance of "obedience, orderliness, unity, and respect for authority" (Jensen, 1998, p. 2).

The *behaviorism* model emerged during the 1950s and 1960s and was characterized by the belief that if a student's behavior could be properly controlled, learning occurs. Championed by B. F. Skinner and John Watson, this model reflected what was known about the brain at that time (Jensen, 1998). This is not an attack on direct instruction because every model of instruction, including the more direct approach, has a place in the teacher's toolbox. We are advocating that teachers experiment with a variety of instructional methods, including direct as well as more collaborative methods of teaching.

Student-Directed Learning and Constructivism

Learning needs to become more student-centered and less teacher-centered—this is the heart of the progressive movement in curriculum, teaching, and subsequent learning. Dewey (1938) stated that "there is no point in the philosophy of progressive education which is sounder than its emphasis upon the importance of the participation of the learner in the formation of purposes which direct his activities in the learning process" (p. 67).

In a student-centered environment, both the curriculum and instruction are focused on the individual in an environment where students are free to be risk takers. Ellis (2004) outlines the tenants of the progressive movement relative to curriculum (Figure 4. 1). The reader is encouraged to take the leap and think about the connections between curriculum and instruction related to the principles of progressivism and student-centered learning.

Teachers need to become the "Guide on the Side" instead of the "Sage on the Stage." This belief is echoed in the constructivist literature. Teaching methods that incorporate the underpinnings of constructivism situate the learner as active rather than passive, and Fosnot (1996) makes the distinction that

> constructivism is a theory of learning, not a description of teaching. No "cookbook teaching style" or pat set of instructional techniques can be abstracted from the theory and proposed as a constructivist approach to teaching. Some general principles of learning derived from constructivism may be helpful to keep in mind, however, as we rethink and reform our educational practices. (p. 29)

Figure 4.1. Elements of a Progressive Curriculum

Emphasis	• Focus on the individual
	• Personal growth and development
	• Learner interest
	• Emphasis on affect
Teaching	• Teacher as facilitator
Learning	• Incidental education
Environment	• Nurturing creativity
	• Stimulating
	• Playful atmosphere
	• Freedom of movement
	• Atmosphere of trust
Assessment	• Learner-initiated
	• Growth oriented
	• Formative emphasis
	• Anecdotal, experiential
	• Noncompetitive

Source: Ellis, A. K. (2004) *Exemplars of Curriculum Theory.* Used with permission.

In the same vein, Gagnon and Collay (2001) indicate that in the constructivist paradigm "learners construct their own knowledge on the basis of interaction with their environment," and that there are assumptions that capture "the heart of constructivist learning," which is

- ♦ physically constructed by learners who are involved in their environment;

- ♦ symbolically constructed by learners who are making their own representations of action;

- ♦ socially constructed by learners who convey their meaning making to others;

- ♦ theoretically constructed by learners who try to explain things they don't understand. (Gagnon & Collay, 2001)

In the constructivist classroom, students are involved in problem-solving activities, "actively constructing knowledge" (O'Neil, 1998, p. 51), and receiving feedback on their work to ensure deeper understanding (Wilson & Cole, 1991).

Differentiated Instruction

Research has cast new light about the way children learn, and no longer can we assume that any one instructional strategy is sufficient to reach *all* learners *all* of the time.

Differentiated instruction is more of a mind-set rather than an instructional model. To differentiate, teachers provide alternate approaches to developing content, the methods used to present content, and the ways in which students show mastery of learning objectives. Given the myriad ability levels of students and the recognition that no two learners learn at the same rate or way, differentiated instruction shows great promise as a way of thinking about teaching and learning. In a classroom where instruction is differentiated, students are offered a variety of ways to learn. According to Tomlinson (1999), differentiated instruction flourishes when

- teachers begin where the students are;
- teachers engage students in instruction through different learning modalities;
- a student competes more against himself or herself than others;
- teachers provide specific ways for each individual to learn;
- teachers use classroom time flexibly;
- teachers are diagnosticians, prescribing the best possible instruction for each student. (p. 2)

For differentiated instruction to work, flexibility is needed to assess student strengths and weaknesses and in designing the means to meet student learning needs.

Walker (1998) indicates that less than 30% of students learn by lecture, and after about 15 minutes, their attention begins to evaporate. This limited attention span, coupled with the need for an enriched learning environment as demonstrated by current brain research, completes a convincing case for using differentiated teaching strategies. Strategies could include Socratic Seminars, cooperative learning, and inquiry. It is not possible within the limitations of this chapter to provide complete information on any one teaching strategy. The following section provides an overview of select instructional strategies.

Instructional Methods

Socratic Seminars

A *Socratic Seminar* is a structured class dialogue in which the teacher and students alike serve as both facilitators and participants. A text for discussion is selected by the teacher and read by both teacher and students. The seminar begins with an opening question designed by the teacher to introduce main themes of the text or possible topics for discussion. This question should be open-ended to encourage discussion.

Following the opening question, students discuss the themes of the text, and they are required to support their positions with passages from within the text. To sustain the momentum of the discussion, the teacher prepares two to five *core questions,* which ask students to take a position on an issue and to support that position with passages from the text. It is important to note that teacher-generated questions for the Socratic Seminar need to be value-free. Students should be encouraged to make and defend their own judgments.

The last phase of the Socratic Seminar consists of a final question that encourages the students to apply what they have learned to the real world. For example, a history class studying World War II might use Chapter 12, "The Road to Munich," from William L. Shirer's *The Rise and Fall of the Third Reich* to investigate how Hitler's dishonesty with various political leaders affected the course of world events. Students could then transfer their newly constructed knowledge of the consequences of deception to student leaders and their roles in school organizations.

Socratic Seminars benefit student learning by

♦ providing opportunity for students to be leaders in their own learning;

♦ requiring students to use higher-order thinking skills;

♦ allowing students to construct knowledge free of value judgments.

To facilitate discussion and to establish that all participants (including the teacher) "hold the same rank," it is recommended that chairs be moved to form a circle. This arrangement also makes eye contact easier (Ball & Brewer, 1996).

Supervision and the Socratic Seminar

For the principal observing a teacher using the Socratic Seminar method, there are types of data that can be recorded and then shared with the teacher. According to Courtright (2003), Socratic Seminar leaders engage learners by actively focusing on the participants and their interactions with other members and the text and subsequent discussion. Figure 4.2 is adapted from Courtright's work to help the supervisor track the work of the teacher using the Socratic Seminar method.

Figure 4.2. Socratic Seminar Classroom Observation Form

Teacher Behaviors   *Notes*

1. Asks a series of questions that give direction to the discussion.

2. Makes sure questions are understood or rephrases them until they are understood.

3. Raises issues that lead to further questions.

4. Asks questions that allow for a range of answers deserving consideration and demanding judgment.

5. Allows for discussion of conflict or differences.

6. Examines answers and draws out implications or reasons.

7. Insists that answers be clear or be rephrased until they are clear.

8. Requests that reasons for answers be given.

9. Does not entertain answers for argument's sake alone.

10. Pursues questions and issues raised by answers.

11. Does not insist upon general agreement to a single answer.

12. Raises all sides of an argument for examination.

Practices active listening:

- Waits 3–5 seconds for a reply
- Accepts student's answer, then requests support: "Interesting answer. Why... ?"
- Redirects the question:
  - "What does... mean?"
  - "How does... differ from... ?"
  - "In what way would... change if... were different?"
  - "Suppose... happened. What then?"
  - "How do you think... was viewed by... ?"
  - "Why do you say... ?"
  - Prompts for more: "Say more about... ?"

Source: Courtright, R. D. (2003). Socratic Inquiry and Seminar Teaching. Winston-Salem/ Forsyth County (NC) Schools http://home.comcast.net/~dededye1/ SOCRATICINQUIRYANDSEMINAR.DOC Used with permission.

Cooperative Learning

Cooperative learning is an instructional model in which students, working in small groups, complete work as a collaborative learning team. The work of a cooperative learning group is structured so that each group member contributes to the completion of the learning activity. Johnson and Johnson (1994) define cooperative learning as

> students working together... to achieve shared learning goals and to complete specific tasks and assignments. These assignments include decision making or problem solving, completing a curriculum unit, writing a report, conducting a survey or experiment, reading a chapter or reference book, learning vocabulary, or answering questions at the end of the chapter. (p. 52)

To this end, the teacher who wants to use the cooperative learning method needs to spend time up front planning for cooperative group activities. Cooperative learning should not be considered a "spur of the moment" method, as students need opportunity and practice with working with one another. For the classroom supervisor as well as the teacher, cooperative learning group work is sometimes seemingly chaotic, with students talking with one another, perhaps even across groups, comparing answers, quizzing one another, or securing materials from bookshelves.

Activity is the norm in cooperative groups. While students are in cooperative groups, the teacher maintains "withitness" (Kounin, 1977) working with students across groups more as a facilitator rather than providing direct instruction. The directions the teacher provides, the monitoring the teacher does within and across groups, and the eye to time on task are essential for cooperative learning to be successful.

Kagan (1992) identifies six essential steps for implementing cooperative learning:

1. *Class building:* Students need to become acquainted with one another prior to being divided into groups.

2. *Team formation:* Students are divided into teams of usually three or four members either by teacher, student, or random selection.

3. *Team building:* Teams become acquainted with one another through ice-breaker activities.

4. *Identity:* After ice-breaker activities, teams develop a team identity with a name or logo.

5. *Cooperative learning structures:* To ensure involvement by all members, learning activities are completed by the team with every member having a specific responsibility (e.g., recorder or researcher).

6. *Group processing and evaluation:* Students, along with the teacher, evaluate each member's contribution. Peer evaluation and self-evaluation are encouraged.

Cooperative learning yields many benefits to student learning: positive interdependence, face-to-face interactions, individual accountability, and development of social and group processing skills (Johnson & Johnson, 1994). According to Sharan and Sharan (1976), cooperative learning is most successful when the role of the teacher changes:

An active planning and learning role for the student necessitates a complementary change in the role of the teacher. From being a dispenser and transmitter of knowledge, he [she] becomes a guide and advisor to students. He [She] helps them investigate issues and clarify and solve problems; but he [she] is not the main source of information. (pp. 4–5)

The Teacher's Role in Cooperative Learning

In cooperative learning, the teacher assumes responsibility for the following activities:

- *Specifying objectives for the lesson:* Both an academic objective and a social skills objective should be specified.

- *Making preinstructional decisions:* These decisions include size of groups, how students will be assigned to groups, what materials will be needed, and how the room will be arranged.

- *Explaining the task and positive interdependence:* The assignment is clearly defined including explanation of required concepts to be used, criteria for success, and individual accountability. Positive interdependence is emphasized.

- *Monitoring students' learning and intervening within the groups:* Through monitoring the group activities, the teacher will be able to determine individual student involvement. When necessary, the teacher intervenes to facilitate completion of task and interaction patterns of the group.

- *Evaluating students' learning and helping students process how well their group functioned:* Both student learning and group interaction are evaluated by the teacher, followed by student evaluation (Johnson & Johnson, 1994).

As a supervisor, feedback could be provided to the teacher by using anecdotal notes across the categories that Johnson and Johnson (1994) identified as landscaped in Figure 4.3.

The Student's Role in Cooperative Learning

Students also have responsibilities to ensure successful implementation of cooperative learning. Johnson and Johnson (1990) conclude that students must:

- get to know and trust one another;
- communicate accurately and unambiguously;
- accept and support one another;
- resolve conflicts constructively. (p. 30)

Figure 4.3. Tracking Teacher Behaviors Promoting Cooperative Learning

	Duration	*Notes*
1. Objectives for the cooperative learning group		
2. Clarity of directions		
3. Monitoring and intervening strategies		
4. Evaluation strategies		
5. Interactions with students		
6. Follow-up instruction		

Johnson and Johnson (1990) identify the following as necessary social skills for cooperative learning: staying with the group, using quiet voices, giving direction to the group's work, encouraging participation, explaining answers, and criticizing ideas without criticizing people. Through monitoring group work, the teacher can help the students learn the necessary social skills needed to focus learning in the cooperative learning model.

In cooperative learning, students can assume a variety of active roles, for example, reader/explainer, checker, and recorder. Within the structure of the cooperative group, the teacher should encourage students to rotate roles to give students an opportunity to serve as the reader/explainer, checker, and recorder.

The supervisor can assist teachers in assessing the work of students, individually or in groups, by collecting data on what students are doing and how students are interacting with one another in cooperative learning groups. Although used to track the participation of college students in the development of unit development, the rubric (Figure 4.4) developed by Frandsen (2003) can be adapted across subject and grade levels to give students feedback about their participation. The principal or peer coach can use Frandsen's rubric to collect data during a classroom observation, and review with the colleague information about student participation and interactions with others.

Figure 4.4. Participation Assessment Rubric

Name	Area	Excellent = 5	Good = 4	Average = 3	Poor = 2	Notes/ Score
	Work	Did a full share of the work	Did an equal share of the work	Did almost as much work as others	Did less work than others	
	Organizing	Took the initiative in helping the group get organized	Worked agreeably with partner(s) concerning times and places to meet	Could be coaxed into meeting with other partner(s)	Did not meet partner(s) at agreed times and places	
	Generating Ideas	Provided many ideas for the unit development	Participated in discussions about unit	Listened to others; on some occasions, made suggestions	Seemed bored with conversations about the unit	
	Cooperative Behaviors	Assisted other partner(s)	Offered encouragement to other partner(s)	Seemed preoccupied with own lessons	Took little pride in own lesson	
	Quality of Work	Work was ready on time or sometimes ahead of time.	Work was ready very close to the agreed time.	Work was usually late but was completed in time to be graded.	Some work never got completed and other partner(s) completed the assignment.	
	Interactions with Group Members	Clearly communicated desires, ideas, personal needs, and feelings	Usually shared feelings and thoughts with other partner(s)	Rarely expressed feelings, preferences	Never spoke up to express excitement and/or frustration	
	Affirmation of Group Members	Expressed frequent appreciation for other group members	Often encouraged and appreciated other partner(s)	Seemed to take the work of others for granted	Group members often wondered, "What is going on here?"	
	Feedback	Gave feedback to others that dignified	Gave feedback in ways that did not offend	Sometimes hurt feelings of others with feedback	Was openly rude when giving feedback	

Source: Frandsen, B. (2003). Participation Rubric for Unit Development. St. Edward's University, Center for Teaching Excellence, Austin, TX. http://www.stedwards.edu/cte/resources/grub.htm Used with permission.

Types of Cooperative Learning

Johnson, Johnson, and Smith (1991) identify three major types of cooperative learning. *Formal cooperative learning* consists of groups that work on assignments over the period of several class periods. *Informal cooperative learning* groups work on tasks for only a class period or less. The membership of these groups is often reformulated. *Cooperative base groups* are heterogeneous groups that can last over a period of several school years and meet formally a day or two per week. The purpose of the cooperative base group is to provide peer support for student learning.

Cooperative learning structures are structures developed to manage classroom routines. *Think-pair-share,* often shortened to TPS, is a popular cooperative learning structure. Students, working in pairs, are asked questions by the teacher. Each student is required to wait (think) three to five seconds before consulting his/her partner (pair), and then each pair communicates its answer to the rest of the class (share). This strategy is helpful in engaging more students in the learning process (Strebe, 1996).

Other cooperative learning structures include *pair reading* and *jigsawing.* Pair reading groups are especially helpful when there is a large amount of materials that need to be covered or the materials under study are complex. Paired reading groups divide the materials to be read and then team members read and share what they have read with group members checking for accuracy and extending the discussion.

Like a puzzle, through the jigsaw technique of cooperative learning, small groups of students each read different materials related to a topic and then become teachers of that material to a different, subsequent smaller group of students. Each person of the jigsaw has a piece of the puzzle, and members of the group rely on each other to contribute a piece of the puzzle.

Assessing Cooperative Learning

When assessing student learning while using cooperative learning, each student should receive his/her own grade. Teacher workload is an argument in favor of group grading; however, Kagan (1995) makes a persuasive argument in supporting the necessity of individual grading. Group grades

♦ hold students accountable for circumstances beyond their control, namely, the performance of classmates;

♦ violate the principle of individual accountability;

♦ create resistance in parents, teachers, and students to cooperative learning;

♦ may be challenged in court. (pp. 70–71)

Supervision and Cooperative Learning

For the principal, supervising during a cooperative learning lesson might be challenging in that often there is a great deal of student interaction and movement as students get into groups and work with one another. To help the principal help teachers to assess cooperative learning, the checklist shown in Figure 4.5, adapted from the work of Candler (2003), is helpful in tracking instruction using the cooperative learning method.

Figure 4.5. Tracking Cooperative Learning

Focus Area	Classroom Observation Notes	Suggested Strategy
Social skills		Teach a new social skill each week. Keep the activities simple and structured
Low motivation of students to participate		Share with students the rationale for using cooperative learning activities... academics, skills for employment. If necessary, switch to structured independent activities, then try again later.
Response to teacher cues (quiet signal, regrouping signal)		Reteach the quiet signal or others; use a reward system to reinforce the desired response.
Following directions		Give directions in bite-sized pieces and model with a team. Write directions on the overhead or a chart.
Uncooperative behavior		Depending on the severity, remove the individuals and switch to seatwork activities while the others are doing cooperative learning activities. Give them a chance to earn their way back into the group in a day or two.
Too noisy but on task		Cue students to acceptable levels of loudness.
Reluctant students		Analyze the structure and make sure you are providing for equal participation. Use structures like round-robin, pairs check, timed-pair-share, and rally table to encourage kids to do their fair share.

Adapted with permission from Laura Candler http://home.att.net/~candlers/resources.htm

Simulations

Simulations are re-creations of real-world situations in which students, through role-play, are given the opportunity to apply content to a given problem. All core content areas (English, social studies, mathematics, and science) are replete with possibilities for simulations. For example, a history class might stage a mock trial; a science class could "race against the clock" in responding to an epidemic; or a mathematics class could use simple probability theory and statistics in a simulation of a research study.

Successful simulations require the following:

♦ *A stated objective:* Tell the students what they are expected to learn from the exercise.

♦ *Clearly defined roles for each student:* State what each student is expected to do and within what limitations (if any).

♦ *Concisely written rules:* Explain what is and is not permitted within the confines of the simulation.

♦ *Discussion questions:* Provide closure for the lesson.

♦ *Specific assessment rubric:* Indicate how student performance will be assessed.

Simulations can be enhanced with field trips, guest speakers, and technology. For example, in a mock trial, a social studies class might visit a local court to gain firsthand knowledge of how a trial proceeds. A biology class that is studying microorganisms could invite a local physician, paramedic, or public health official to discuss disease control. Students in English classes can enhance simulations by comparing a play to its motion picture counterpart prior to creating their own screenplay based on a selection they have read.

Simulations also provide an excellent platform for designing interdisciplinary lessons. A mock trial can involve mathematics and science classes as "expert witnesses," journalism classes are "press pools," and debate students can be excellent coaches for attorneys. Preparing for simulations can be a time-consuming process, but, the benefits to student learning are well worth the effort.

Inquiry

The inquiry model of instruction has its roots in the science classroom. According to Suchman (1962), the purpose of inquiry is to "help children develop a set of skills and a broad schema for the investigation of causal relationships" (p. 3). The inquiry method consists of four main activities:

1. *Searching:* the planned and controlled collection of data

2. *Data processing:* the organization of data to discern any patterns that may be present

3. *Discovery:* the process of seeing how data fits together

4. *Verification:* the "check" on the process of forming conclusions. (pp. 5–20)

Using the inquiry method, students are presented with an open-ended assignment that becomes the foundation for student inquiry into learning objectives. For example, a mathematics teacher might use inquiry to introduce π (the symbol for the circumference of a circle divided by its diameter—see Figure 4.6).

Figure 4.6. Diameter and Circumference of a Circle

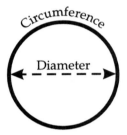

With students working in teams, have them measure the circumference and diameter of every circular object in the classroom. Next, the students could build a chart giving each set of measurements and their quotients. Students discover the secret ($\pi = 3.14$) because the last column of the chart should repeat an approximation of this number (see Figure 4.7). The closer the approximation in the last column, the more accurate the students' measurements are.

Figure 4.7. Summary Chart of Measurements

Item	*Diameter (D)*	*Circumference (C)*	*C ÷ D*
Coffee Mug	3"	9.4"	3.13
Magic Marker	.75"	2.4"	3.20
UHF TV Antenna	7"	22"	3.143
12 ounce Soda Can	2.3"	7.2"	3.13
Wall Clock	16"	50.2	3.14

In this example, these students would, in part, be developing a problem to solve, collecting and organizing data related to the problem, analyzing data to solve the problem, and drawing inferences about the data to solve the problem. Very much as in the cooperative learning method, the inquiry instructional method situates the student as the center of learning by promoting

♦ generation of knowledge;

♦ higher-order thinking skills;

♦ integration of knowledge as students organize and analyze data in a variety of ways (maps, graphs, charts);

♦ creative problem solving.

The Teacher's Role in the Inquiry Model

Inquiry is a student-driven instructional model. Suchman (1962) established three main tasks for teachers when using the inquiry model:

1. Establish and maintain procedures students are to follow.

2. Make new information available to students when needed.

3. Guide the development of skills and strategies of students.

The Phases of the Inquiry Model

Joyce and Weil (1996) identify five phases of the inquiry model. In phase 1, the students encounter the problem. After the teacher introduces the problem, students begin phase 2, verification through data gathering, by asking yes–no questions to learn more about the problem. In phase 3, students perform two tasks: exploration and direct testing. Exploration requires students to begin adding or deleting information from the data that they collected in phase 2. After direct testing, the students observe and record changes that occurred as a result of the exploration task. Phase 4 requires students to form an explanation or theory based on data collected in phases 2 and 3. In phase 5, students analyze the process through which they formulated their explanation.

Teaching Inquiry:
What Teachers Need to Know

Suchman (1962) described four essentials for successful teaching using the inquiry model:

1. *Concrete problems that are immediately intelligible to the learner:* Students need to be able to understand the problem with minimum explanation from the teacher.

2. *Freedom to perform data-gathering operations:* Learner control over how data are gathered and analyzed facilitates learner autonomy.

3. *A responsive environment:* Necessary data need to be abundantly available to the learners.

4. *Elimination of extrinsic rewards:* The sole motivation for inquiry should be to "find out why." (p. 127)

Supervision and the Inquiry Method

To help the principal assist teachers in assessing their efforts using the inquiry method of instruction, the following checklist can help encourage discussion after a classroom observation (Figure 4.8).

Figure 4.8. Tracking Inquiry During a Classroom Observation

Tenets of the Inquiry Model	*Classroom Observation Notes*
1. Problem or question of importance is established.	
2. The problem or question is manageable.	
3. Students generate tentative answers and engage in making educated guesses.	
4. Students examine information and search for relationships across data sources.	
5. Students are engaged in collecting and analyzing data, noting similarities and differences and finding trends and patterns.	
6. Students evaluate evidence.	
7. Students develop and then test a hypothesis.	

Enhancing Instructional Methods

Learning Centers

The use of learning centers has long been a staple at the elementary level. In contrast, relatively few high school teachers have included this approach as part of their instructional repertoire. Examples of activities for high school learning centers might include

- ◆ devices for measuring and calculating in a geometry class;

- ◆ listening centers in a foreign language class;

- ◆ materials and directions for the completion of a project for a home economics, art, or industrial arts class;

- ◆ equipment for short experiments in a biology class;

- ◆ packets containing short simulations of diplomatic problems in a history class. (Canady & Rettig, 1995, p. 234)

Learning centers can be used as a *transition* strategy. Students might visit two or three learning centers on the way from one major learning activity to another. Learning centers are also effective as enrichment for gifted or talented students (Winebrenner, 1992) and provide additional practice for students who might need extra assistance.

Technology-Based Lessons

Technology offers a plethora of exciting instructional strategies for teachers and students. Through the magic of videotape, students can watch and interact with the major events of World War II instead of filling in worksheets about them. Graphics calculators in an algebra class can help bring to life the connection of equations and graphs to "real life" applications. With Internet access, a German class might take a "virtual field trip" to Berlin, a business mathematics class could track investments, and students in a history class might construct their family histories.

Here are some tips for using technology in the classroom:

- ◆ *Advanced planning:* Ensure needed equipment is available and that necessary background learning has been completed.

- ◆ *State the learning objective:* Communicate what the student is expected to learn from the activity.

- ◆ *Clear instructions:* Ensure students know exactly what to do and in what sequence.

◆ *Learning curve considerations:* Make sure students know how to operate necessary equipment and software.

◆ *Follow-up questions/activity:* Reinforce learning by providing students an activity that will encourage them to reflect on their learning.

◆ *Assessment:* Decide how you will assess student performance and how students will be involved in assessment (if at all).

Puzzles, Games, and Manipulatives

Puzzles and games can enhance any teacher's arsenal of instructional strategies. They can be icebreakers at the beginning of class, acting as "downtime" learning between more intense learning activities or as review at the end of a class period or unit. Puzzles are also easily embedded in other instructional strategies. For example, a history teacher could reinforce a lesson on the Civil War by developing a crossword puzzle in which the answers are Civil War generals or battles. Also, many popular board games are now available in foreign language editions. Formats of familiar television programs such as *Jeopardy!* are especially useful as review for assessments. Logic puzzles can be excellent tools for practicing problem-solving or critical-thinking skills.

For visual learners, manipulatives can be helpful tools for students. Algebra tiles, for example, are used to depict quadratic equations using square and rectangular plastic pieces. When the pieces are assembled, students not only visualize the equation, but by examining its component blocks, students may also visualize its component factors.

Before moving the discussion to differentiated methods of assessment, the reader is asked to reflect on what we do know about instruction and student engagement. Black (2003, p. 7) reports that teachers who engage students do so because they do the following:

◆ Represent curriculum content appropriately.

◆ Expect students to help define topics and determine how they can be studied.

◆ Link content to students' prior knowledge and experiences.

◆ Ensure that students are mentally engaged in all activities and assignments.

◆ Allow students to initiate and adapt learning activities and projects.

◆ Form instructional groups that work to achieve learning goals.

◆ Choose suitable instructional materials for lessons and encourage students to select resources that will help them learn.

♦ Teach highly coherent, well-planned, and well-paced lessons that include time for student reflection.

(Reprinted with permission from *American School Board Journal*, December 2003.
Copyright 2003 National School Boards Association. All Rights Reserved.)

Black (2003) also reports, students are more likely to be engaged when
teachers pay close individual attention to their interests and the ways they
learn. Students stay engaged when teachers create lessons centered on 'big
ideas' and design assignments at the correct level of difficulty—not too easy
and not impossibly difficult—so students are challenged but still able to succeed. (p. 13)

Differentiated Assessment

The use of diverse teaching methods necessitates the use of equally diverse
assessment techniques. Although pencil-and-paper tests can still be useful for
evaluating student mastery of some skills, using alternative assessment strategies permits students with diverse learning styles to demonstrate what they
have learned. In Chapter 5, we discuss learning and, by extension, assessment
of learning vis-à-vis brain research, multiple intelligences, and learning styles.

The debate about the use of standardized testing falls outside the scope of
this book; however, traditional assessments (pen and paper), standardized assessments, and authentic assessments all have their place in the classroom. The
real issue is what role assessment plays in examining the curriculum and the instruction. According to McMillan (2000),

> just as assessment impacts student learning and motivation, it also in-
> fluences the nature of instruction in the classroom.... When assess-
> ment is integrated with instruction it informs teachers about what ac-
> tivities and assignments will be most useful, what level of teaching is
> most appropriate, and how summative assessments provide diagnos-
> tic information. For instance, during instruction activities informal,
> formative assessment helps teachers know when to move on, when to
> ask more questions, when to give more examples, and what re-
> sponses to student questions are most appropriate. Standardized test
> scores, when used appropriately, help teachers understand student
> strengths and weaknesses to target further instruction. (p. 9,
> http://PAREonline.net/getvn.asp?v=7&n=8)

The work of Stiggins (1994) can help teachers and administrators talk about
assessment by posing questions to guide the work of assessing learning based
on the purpose, namely, what are you trying to assess and why.

♦ What concept, skill, or knowledge am I trying to assess?

- ◆ What should my students know?

- ◆ At what level should my students be performing?

- ◆ What type of knowledge is being assessed: reasoning, memory, or process? (Stiggins, 1994)

Teaching that is differentiated reaches out to all students, and this type of instruction requires assessment that is authentic. Assessment is authentic if the very assessments are embedded within learning experiences from start to finish. In a sense, the assessment is part of the instructional plan, with the teacher engaging students in a variety of learning opportunities that increase student participation in a variety of ways. See Chapter 5, Figure 5.2, which explores assessments that capitalize on multiple intelligences. More authentic assessment strategies could include portfolios, demonstrations, and research projects.

Portfolios

A portfolio is a collection of artifacts such as essays, drawings, letters, and posters that demonstrate that a student has mastered an objective. Portfolios are particularly useful for assessing progress over an extended period such as an entire grading period. As alternative assessment, portfolios offer several advantages over pencil-and-paper tests. According to Brown (1997), portfolios

- ◆ provide teachers with important information for diagnosing student weaknesses;

- ◆ help students see gaps in their own learning;

- ◆ involve students in the assessment of their learning. (p. 3)

Murphy (1997) believes that an important quality of portfolio assessment is that it is both formative and summative. Given the ongoing (formative) nature of portfolio construction, the development of the portfolio allows teachers and students to diagnose and remediate weaknesses as learning occurs instead of waiting until the very end of a unit, quarter, or semester. To this end, adjustments to instructional and learning activities can be made. In the long term, the development of portfolios can be extended over more than one year. For example, students in English I could transport their portfolios to English II and beyond.

The use of the portfolio over an extended period can provide a powerful view of learning for both the student and the teacher. Instruction can be enhanced with informed modifications made through the results gleaned from examining the content of student portfolios.

Portfolio examination can provide opportunities for teachers to conduct action research about their teaching and its impact on student gains in learning after the efforts of instruction. Student work should reflect content, instruction, analysis, and interpretation. After reviewing student work, teachers can analyze cumulative gains in students' progress against instructional approaches.

To build on the English I portfolio example, the portfolio, if used by several teachers at the same grade level, can help assess the overall curriculum and its impact. Through this type of action research—the auditing techniques suggested in this chapter—teachers can assess course content, instructional strategies, learning activities, pacing, and assessment techniques. By examining these areas, teachers will be able to learn from one another and, through dialogue, become better teachers.

Demonstrations

Demonstrations have traditionally been the domain of electives such as music, drama, and the industrial arts. However, demonstrations can be effective assessment tools of simulations and cooperative learning across all core courses. For example, following a unit on area, a geometry teacher could have students demonstrate mastery of content by developing and presenting an original practical application problem such as determining the area of an irregularly shaped lake. The presentation should include necessary calculations and a narrative explaining what type of practitioner (e.g., surveyor, architect) would need to know how to solve this problem and why.

Research Projects

Research projects can provide useful data for student assessment in a variety of settings. In place of a pencil-and-paper test, a physical science teacher might have students collect and test soil samples from the surrounding area to demonstrate understanding of local erosion problems. Included in this project could be a formal paper reporting the results, a class presentation or demonstration, and peer as well as teacher assessment of a presentation or demonstration.

Suggested Readings

Baloche, L. A. (1998). *The cooperative classroom: Empowering learning.* Upper Saddle River, NJ: Prentice Hall.

Benjamin, A. (2002). *Differentiated instruction: A guide for middle and high school teachers.* Larchmont, NY: Eye on Education.

Benjamin, A. (2003). *Differentiated instruction: A guide for elementary school teachers.* Larchmont, NY: Eye On Education.

Brooks, J. G., & Brooks, M. G. (1993). *The case for constructivist classrooms.* Alexandria, VA: Association for Supervision and Curriculum Development.

Brown, A. L., & Palinscar, A. S. (1989). Guided, cooperative learning and individual knowledge acquisition. In L. B. Resnick (Ed.), *Knowing, learning, and instruction* (pp. 393–451). Hillsdale, NJ: Erlbaum.

Johnson, D. W., Johnson, R. T., & Holubec, E. J. (1993). *Circles of learning: Cooperation in the classroom* (4th ed.). Edina, MN: Interaction Book.

Joyce, B., Weil, M., & Calhoun, E. (2000). *Models of teaching* (6th ed.). Needham Heights, MA: Allyn & Bacon.

Moeller, V. J., & Moeller, M. V. (2002). *Socratic seminars and literature circles for middle and high school English.* Larchmont, NY: Eye On Education.

Popham, W. J. (1995). *Classroom assessment: What teachers need to know.* Needham Heights, MA: Allyn & Bacon.

Slavin, R. E. (1995). *Cooperative learning: Theory, research and practice* (2nd. ed.). Needham Heights, MA: Allyn & Bacon.

Stiggins, R. J. (1994). *Student-centered classroom assessment.* NY: Macmillan.

Tomlinson, C. A. (2003). *Fulfilling the promise of the differentiated classroom: Strategies and tools for responsive teaching.* Alexandria, VA: Association for Supervision and Curriculum Development.

5

Brain Research, Multiple Intelligences, and Learning Styles

In this Chapter...

♦ Overview of differentiated instruction

♦ Teacher-centered paradigm

♦ Student-centered learning

♦ The human brain

♦ Multiple intelligences

♦ Learning styles

♦ Using brain research, multiple intelligences, and learning styles to differentiate instruction

♦ Supervision to support the use of brain research, multiple intelligences, and learning styles

With the passage of federal and state legislation, new levels of accountability for educators have arrived. For example, with *No Child Left Behind*, individual students, classrooms, and school sites are required to show *adequate yearly progress* (AYP) as measured on criterion-referenced tests. In some states, educator evaluations are now being connected to student results on these tests. It is natural, under these circumstances, for educators to concentrate their efforts in preparing students for "the test." However, educators are still charged with the responsibility to present the required curriculum in ways that reach all learners in the classroom. This charge has created the need for teachers to differentiate instruction and for principals to supervise and support teachers' efforts.

For the teacher, differentiated instruction means using a variety of pedagogically sound strategies to involve all students actively in their own learning, regardless of learning styles or abilities. In a real sense, teachers need to become "pedagogical tailors," customizing the "fit" of instruction for each learner—a daunting task, to be sure. If teachers are to teach differently, they will need learning opportunities tailored to their needs. Providing these opportunities falls to the principal. The successful principal brings to the table a deep knowledge base of techniques of differentiated instruction based on current research in brain function and cognition, multiple intelligences, and learning styles. Supervising teachers using these techniques requires the principal to recognize these techniques in the context of instruction, regardless of his or her level of familiarity with the content or grade level.

What Is Differentiated Instruction?

Differentiated instruction refers to a teacher's ability to use a "variety of classroom practices that accommodate differences in students' learning styles, interests, prior knowledge, socialization needs, and comfort zones" (Benjamin, 2002, p. 1). Differentiating instruction begins with developing an understanding of students as individuals, and then incorporating that understanding in all phases of teaching—lesson planning, delivery of instruction, and assessment of the resulting student learning. Teachers develop this understanding of students by learning about each student as an individual in terms of interests, prior learning experiences, and personal history.

The Supervisor's Score Card

♦ Student data are available to teachers (e.g., past achievement data such as test results, report cards, progress reports, etc.).

♦ Grade-level and/or team-meeting time is available to teachers at the beginning and end of the year (teachers should be given time and opportunity to discuss students passing from one grade to another at key points during the year).

♦ Support staff (school nurse, counselor, and others) are given the opportunity to share information about students with teaching staff.

♦ Time is allotted for teachers to confer with students and parents.

Instructional decisions based on this kind of student examination need to be grounded in a clear understanding of current research in the areas of brain functioning, multiple intelligences, and learning styles and modalities. In short, differentiated instruction is based on the idea that students, not teachers, are at the center of instruction. The remainder of this chapter examines not the models of instruction but the platform from which differentiated instruction springs—brain research, multiple intelligences, and learning styles.

The Human Brain: Cultivating the Potential for Learning

During the 1990s, numerous studies were conducted on how the human brain functions. Unfortunately for teachers and administrators, these research studies did not customarily identify specific implications for teaching and learning, leaving educational professionals to interpret brain research and to decide how (if at all) specific findings should impact classroom practices. This section offers the reader a primer on how the brain works, some specific findings of brain research, and a few recommendations about brain research that may inform teaching and learning.

The human brain is composed of billions of cells. Two types most central to the study of learning are neurons and glial cells. Neurons are composed of dendrites, an axon, and the cell body. Dendrites are the receptive surfaces of neurons that make possible the reception of information and the axon is the sender of information. The axon is coated with a substance called myelin, which acts as insulation and facilitates the transmission of messages. Neurons "talk" to each other through chemicals called neurotransmitters that flow from the axon of one neuron to the dendrites of another through spaces called synapses. Glial cells, whose name means glue, act as a support system for the neurons, in effect nurturing the neurons (Sprenger, 1999).

Learning is traditionally assessed on the basis of memory. Teachers seek to make judgments concerning what information can be recalled and represented with pencil on paper. Berninger and Richards (2002) explain that the brain's many memory mechanisms can be divided into short-term memory (STM) and long-term memory (LTM), and they identify four processes required for a person to be able to integrate these memory mechanisms:

1. Coding in STM
2. Consolidation (converting information for storage in LTM)
3. Storage in LTM
4. Retrieval. (pp. 126–127)

Because of severe limitations in capacity and duration, information stored in STM is lost if it is not converted and stored in LTM. Just as one remembers a telephone number just long enough to place a call, too many students remember content just long enough to regurgitate it on a test. Baddeley (1986) argued for a fifth memory process called working memory. Working memory, involving both STM and LTM, is believed to provide the basis for high-level cognitive processes such as thinking and problem solving.

Relevant Findings from Brain Research

Wolfe and Brandt (1998) identify four findings from brain research that seem particularly relevant to teaching and learning.

1. The brain changes physically as a result of experience.

2. Intelligence is not fixed at birth.

3. There are certain sensitive periods, or "windows of opportunity," for learning.

4. Learning is strongly influenced by emotion. (pp. 11–13)

The Changing Brain

Over time, the human brain does change. A lack of change would make adapting to new environments difficult if not impossible, while unconstrained change could result in chaos. The controlled way in which the human brain changes is called plasticity (Berninger & Richards, 2002). Research suggests that an enriched learning environment is important to supporting positive change in the human brain as neurotransmitters and dendrites become more active. Figure 5.1 illustrates characteristics, according to Wesson (2002), of an enriched learning environment and gives cues to the supervisor to check for the application of instructional methods and classroom procedures that acknowledge the way the brain works and reinforces an environment that supports student learning.

Figure 5.1. Brain Enriched Learning Environments

Creating Learning Environments that are both

"Brain-Considerate" and "Enriched"
(Adapted from Marian Diamond's *Magic Trees of the Mind*)

♦ Encourage learners to *ask questions and explore* (not just "allow" them to ask questions and explore.)

♦ Provide a steady source of *positive emotional support* and stimulation. "Catch" students being good. ("I saw what you did, Juan, *and I like it!*")

♦ Stimulate *all* of the senses. Elaborate neural connections develop as a direct response to one's life experiences.

♦ Keep the learning environment *free from undue pressure* and stress. Pleasurable "eustress" is encouraged rather than "distress."

♦ Offer an abundance of novel, fun, interesting, *comprehensible* (developmentally appropriate) *challenges.*

♦ Give learners numerous opportunities to *select the kinds of learning efforts* they will pursue and encourage them to modify their choices after they have been made to promote flexibility in thinking.

♦ Provide a *nutritious diet* with proteins, vitamins, water, and calories.

♦ Cultivate a broad range of emerging talents and interests (physical, mental, linguistic, mathematical, aesthetic, social, emotional, etc.)

♦ Allow the learner to be an *active* participant—a leader and a "doer"—rather than regularly taking on the role of a passive observer.

♦ Create an environment where a wide variety of *social interactions* is essential during a significant percentage of the time while students are engaged in learning activities.

♦ Ensure that *physical movement* takes place, because it plays a vitally important role in the formation of neural circuitry, which can promote learning.

♦ Begin a learning experience with simple *whole-body* integrative movements; the students will then learn more easily. Movement continues to activate the neural wiring throughout the brain, making *the entire body a catalyst in the learning process.*

♦ Movement increases blood flow to the cerebral cortex and profoundly improves cognitive development. It aids in creativity, helps stress management and growth, and promotes mental and physical health.

♦ Promote an atmosphere where the whole *learning experience itself is always fun!* (The joy of youthful discovery is forever encouraged.)

Source: Kenneth Wesson (2002). *Creating Learning environments that are "Brain-Considerate" and "Enriched."* http://www.sciencemaster.com/wesson/pdfs/enriched_learning.pdf Used with permission.

The opposite is also true. Dendrites that have not been put to use die off. This process, known as *pruning,* takes place in impoverished learning environments (D'Arcangelo, 1998). Cultivating an enriched learning environment is essential, and Wolfe and Brandt (1998) indicate, "We educators are either growing dendrites or letting them wither and die. The trick is to determine what constitutes an enriched environment" (p. 11).

The Supervisor's Scorecard

Focus on Instruction to Create an Enriched Learning Environment

♦ Students are given time to process information.

♦ Students are provided with multiple opportunities to apply knowledge in unique and differing ways.

♦ Students are challenged to learn.

♦ Feedback is given to students to extend knowledge.

♦ New knowledge connects to prior knowledge.

♦ Teachers use higher-order questioning strategies using Bloom's Higher-Order

Questioning that spans lower order to higher order items:

- Knowledge
- Comprehension
- Application
- Analysis
- Synthesis
- Evaluation

The Development of Intelligence

The plasticity of the brain suggests that intelligence is not fixed at birth. Research by Ramey and Ramey (1996) argues that children who are at risk at an early age can, with proper intervention, experience an increase in their intelligence quotients. This finding suggests that classroom environments for children, especially younger ones, need to focus on developmental learning activities. The ability to increase intelligence is further suggested by Feuerstein's (1980) theory that intelligence is a function of experience and Gardner's (1993) theory of multiple intelligences. In part, Gardner defines intelligence as having "a characteristic pattern of development" (1993, p. 242).

Windows of Opportunity

Bruer (1998) argues that brain research has identified certain sensitive periods or windows of opportunity in which children experience rapid brain development. According to Wolfe and Brandt (1998), "During the period from birth to age 10, the number of synaptic connections continues to rise rapidly, then begins to drop and continues to decline slowly into adult life" (p. 12). Using positron emission tomography (PET) scans, Chugani (1999) calculated average brain energy use at various ages and concluded that peak synapse production times during the prepubescent years are also peak learning years. Bruer (1998) asserts that there are different critical periods for different types of skills:

> For humans, even in early developing systems like vision, these periods can last until early childhood. For language, the critical period for learning phonology—learning to speak without an accent—ends in early childhood, but the critical period for learning a language's grammar does not end until around age 16. (p. 16)

It should be noted, however, that for some skills there does not appear to be such a window: "When it comes to other skills, such as math or music, there is virtually no evidence for learning windows at all" (Kluger & Park, 2001, p. 54).

Emotion and Learning

Another important finding about learning is the strong connection between learning and emotion. Emotional involvement is prerequisite to learning; emotion is the engine that propels attention, which, in turn, makes learning and memory possible. Sylwester (1995, p. 72) identifies emotion as key to learning: "We know emotion is very important to the educative process because it drives attention, which drives learning and memory."

The normal activity of the human brain is roughly analogous to a mountain range with peaks and valleys. Jensen, in an interview with D'Arcangelo, explains,

> the normal human brain works in periods of high levels of attention, followed by periods of low levels of attention. The brain needs downtime…. If you're introducing something fairly new and complex to students, they'll probably need more downtime more often than if you are reviewing material that they already know pretty well. (D'Arcangelo, 1998, pp. 24–25)

During downtime, the brain strengthens its hold on new knowledge. It appears that strategically placed downtime and the use of multiple instructional methods can help increase retention of what is learned.

Wolfe and Brandt (1998) believe that emotion plays a dual role in learning. First, a strong emotional attachment to an experience leads to a stronger memory of the experience. Second, if emotion is too strong (e.g., when the brain perceives a threat), learning can be decreased. These two assertions, if true, lend credence to the development of instruction and learning activities that engage students in work that is student centered. Students need to be engaged in their learning; they need to have a positive emotional experience with the following:

- Instruction
- The teacher
- Fellow classmates
- The activities that promote learning and mastery

Recommendations for Teaching and Learning

Perhaps the most debated aspect of brain research is deciding how this new knowledge should impact teaching and learning in the classroom. An examination of recent public school professional development programs reveals the widespread interest expressed by educators in brain research. Although brain research has many proponents, some recommend prudence in interpreting findings. Wolfe and Brandt (1998) exhort educators to "critically read and analyze the [brain] research in order to separate the wheat from the chaff" (p. 10). Jorgenson (2003) advises educators to make "sure… applied practices are sifted from speculation, interpretations, and assumptions based loosely on scientific research" because "[educators'] professionalism, and millions of children, depend upon it" (p. 368).

A careful consideration of relevant findings in the brain research suggests that traditional, direct instruction tends to support short-term learning. Recommendations that seem to hold the greatest promise for increasing student learning include

- using multiple teaching strategies;
- teaching for long-term memory;
- actively involving students in learning.

Brain plasticity and development of intelligence suggest that students are capable of much more than passive, rote learning. Active teaching strategies such as cooperative learning and inquiry require students to learn more than just content; critical thinking skills, problem-solving skills, and intrapersonal skills are learned as well. The use of multiple teaching strategies also allows the teacher to appeal to students' emotions in a variety of ways. Chapter 4 examines teaching strategies and Chapter 6 examines the characteristics of children across grades PreK–12, and the reader is encouraged to consult these chapters for further elaboration.

Teachers also need to teach for long-term memory. Wolfe (2001) supports the use of elaborative rehearsal instead of rote rehearsal in learning. Rote rehearsal (e.g., memorizing definitions and addition facts) does not typically engage the students emotionally. As a result, learning is short term. Elaborative rehearsal encompasses strategies that require the students to elaborate on the information at hand and to find ways making it relevant to them. These strategies can include finding solutions to real-life problems or creating and performing in simulations. These types of learning activities set the stage for teachers to assess learning more holistically—and more authentically. Teachers who use multiple teaching strategies and alternative forms of assessment are more likely to have in their classrooms students who are active learners, as opposed to passive receptors.

The Supervisor's Scorecard

Emotion and learning are enhanced when teachers

♦ Create a sense of surprise and mystery

♦ Use humor

♦ Respect students

♦ Create a safe, fault-free learning environment

♦ Connect prior learning to new learning

♦ Give learners choices about learning

♦ Pay attention to the learning environment (clean, orderly) and its atmosphere (desks in semicircles or in a U-shape, student artifacts displayed)

♦ Challenge students without exerting threats or pressuring students into learning

♦ Engage learners in intensive dialogue (e.g., the Socratic Seminar—see Chapter 4) and engage learners as equals (e.g., forms of cooperative learning—see Chapter 4).

Source: Adapted from Caine and Caine (1997).

Multiple Intelligences

For more than a century, intelligence has been viewed as a singular entity. In 1983, Howard Gardner challenged this belief in his landmark work *Frames of Mind: The Theory of Multiple Intelligences,* in which he identified seven intelligences; and in 1999, Gardner examined three potential new intelligences in his book, *Intelligence Reframed: Multiple Intelligences for the 21st Century.* Gardner's work included a list of criteria for identifying capacities to include "an identifiable core, a characteristic pattern of development, a number of specific end-states, neurological representation, and discernible patterns of breakdown" (Gardner, 1993, p. 242). Here are the criteria, according to Gardner, and as reported in *Tapping into Multiple Intelligences* (n.d.):

- All human beings possess all… intelligences in varying amounts.
- Each person has a different intellectual composition.
- We can improve education by addressing the multiple intelligences of our students.
- These intelligences are located in different areas of the brain and can work either independently or together.
- These intelligences may define the human species. (http://www.thirteen.org/edonline/concept2class/month1/)

One way to differentiate instruction is to acknowledge the multiple intelligences of students and to teach to these intelligences. The following descriptions of the multiple intelligences can help the principal work with teachers toward teaching to the multiple intelligences as a means to reach more students, more of the time.

Linguistic Intelligence

According to Gardner, poetry best illustrates linguistic intelligence. Three domains of language are identified: semantics, phonology, and syntax. *Semantics* refers to the examination of the meanings of words, *phonology* describes the sounds or musical quality of words, and *syntax* is a collective term for the rules that govern the order of words and their inflections. In Gardner's view, language performs four major functions: rhetorical (to convince), mnemonic (to remember), explanatory (to explain), and metalinguistic (to reflect on language itself). Linguistic intelligence is primarily vocal, not written.

Musical Intelligence

The core components of musical intelligence are pitch, rhythm, and timbre. *Pitch* defines the auditory frequency at which sound occurs; *Rhythm,* the relationship of a series of pitches over the continuum of time; and timbre, the qualities of a given tone. Musical intelligence, according to Gardner, is the earliest of the intelligences to emerge and is closely linked to emotion.

Music has its own syntax, from which a composer is able to build musical compositions. Persons with high levels of musical intelligence are able to discern patterns such as scales and arpeggios that can be deeply embedded in composition. Through commonalties such as ratios and patterns, musical intelligence is closely related to logical-mathematical intelligence.

Logical-Mathematical Intelligence

Logical-mathematical intelligence is the first intelligence identified by Gardner that is not auditory in nature. It is built on a platform of quantity and sequence. Early recognition of logical-mathematical intelligence can be manifested in the ability to collect and to quantify groups of objects into sets. The highest level of logical-mathematical intelligence is the ability to transfer concrete operations such as counting to abstract problem solving. The most central gift within logical-mathematical intelligence is the ability to manipulate long chains of reasoning.

Spatial Intelligence

Spatial intelligence is described as the ability

to perceive the visual world accurately, to perform transformations and modifications upon one's initial perceptions, and to be able to re-create aspects of one's visual experience, even in the absence of relevant physical stimuli. (Gardner, 1993, p. 173)

Spatial intelligence is exhibited in activities such as problem solving, the visual arts, and games such as chess. The anticipation of future moves depends on a special type of visual memory.

Bodily-Kinesthetic Intelligence

Bodily-kinesthetic intelligence is perhaps best demonstrated by the art of mimes. All communication with the mime's audience is dependent on physical motion. Another mature form of bodily-kinesthetic intelligence is dance. Bodily-kinesthetic intelligence has two components: movement of the body itself and the manipulation of objects.

Interpersonal Intelligence

Interpersonal intelligence is the ability to discern different feelings, motivations, and temperaments in other people. Levels of this intelligence range from a small child discerning basic differences in people to adults reading the intentions of other people. Examples of interpersonal intelligence include a salesperson closing a deal, a politician soliciting support for a project, and a teacher speaking with parents.

Intrapersonal Intelligence

Intrapersonal intelligence is the ability to discern one's own feelings. At its most basic level, intrapersonal intelligence is the ability that allows a person to withdraw one's hand from a hot burner. At is highest level, this ability is revealed through introspective writers, and therapists who help others discern differences in highly complex sets of feelings. Gardner refers to the intrapersonal and interpersonal intelligences as personal intelligences. The personal intelligences are different from other intelligences in that these types of intelligences are

- difficult to track;
- firmly linked to each other;
- easily misdiagnosed;
- more strongly rewarded;
- encouraged more often.

In *Intelligence Reframed,* Gardner (1999) considered the possibility of three new intelligences: naturalistic, spiritual, and existential. Gardner concluded that naturalistic intelligence should be included as the eighth intelligence. Naturalistic intelligence is man's ability to perceive differences in living things and to interpret and extrapolate meaning from other features of the natural world such as rock formations, waterfalls, and clouds. This intelligence is beneficial in diverse endeavors such as landscape architecture, weather forecasting, and hunting.

Gardner dismissed spiritual intelligence as a new intelligence by his definition because of the problematic nature of having cognitive discussions about and the connotations of the word *spiritual.* Turning his attention to the possibility of adding existential intelligence as new intelligence, Gardner (1999) expressed reservation about adding a ninth intelligence. Although scoring admirably on his criteria for a new intelligence, Gardner was only willing to classify existential intelligence as the "8½ intelligence" (p. 66).

Given the press for learning that encourages students to use their "multiple intelligences," the supervisor needs to be ready to assist teachers in developing a sense of how to develop assessments that capitalize on the intelligences. A variety of assessments that use the multiple intelligences is presented in Figure 5.2. However, we take the stand that the teacher and the supervisor will only be limited by their imaginations and should seek to explore assessments that make sense and that align with curricular goals while simultaneously incorporating both instruction and assessment that capitalizes on the multiple intelligences.

Figure 5.2. Helping Teachers Think
About Multiple Intelligences and Assessment

Intelligence	Mathematics	Language Arts	Social Studies	Science
Linguistic (the intelligence of words)	Keep a journal for an extended time in which students chronicle math applications in everyday life.	Write a poem, fable, myth, short story, play, or news article about a current event. Then students tell their story to the class.	Create a story to explain a current event or an event from history.	Write a news story about the science fair; craft an abstract detailing the results from an experiment.
Logical-Mathematical (the intelligence of numbers and reasoning)	Collect and interpret data from activities in the school (e.g., football statistics, food drive).	Develop a timeline to chronicle literature during a specified era.	Develop a timeline to represent an historical period.	Conduct experiments during science labs and graph data using computer applications (e.g., spreadsheet, graphs, bars, histograms).
Spatial (the intelligence of pictures and images)	Chart, graph, and map numbers and shapes. Using the principles of geometry, build to scale a room, a new gym, or some other part of a building.	Rewrite the ending of a book and make a video of the ending with students acting out the new ending.	Create a collage from art reprints of work from specific periods (e.g., Desert Storm) or of current events (use magazine covers, newspaper clips).	Make a slide show of a dissection; use technology to virtually dissect a frog.
Bodily-Kinesthetic (the intelligence of the whole body and the hands)	Create applications where students are required to measure rooms to determine how much carpet would need to be ordered, gallons of paint needed to paint classrooms, wallpaper to order.	After writing a play, have students perform the play.	Select moments in history for students to recreate (e.g., immigrants arriving at Ellis Island during the depression).	Encourage students to build models such as the solar system.
Musical (the intelligence of tone, rhythm, and timbre)	Write and then sing a rap song of the times tables.	Read a poem and identify beats (e.g., iambic pentameter).	Listen to music of a particular era, analyzing lyrics.	Students write a song that could be used as a mnemonic for learning the different levels of classification (e.g., Kingdom, Phylum).

Intelligence	Mathematics	Language Arts	Social Studies	Science
Linguistic (the intelligence of words)	Keep a journal for an extended time in which students chronicle math applications in everyday life.	Write a poem, fable, myth, short story, play, or news article about a current event. Then students tell their story to the class.	Create a story to explain a current event or an event from history.	Write a news story about the science fair; craft an abstract detailing the results from an experiment.
Interpersonal (the intelligence of social interactions)	Students start a pretend business and have them work cooperatively to determine what materials and personnel they will need for their business and how much money they need to get started.	Stage a classroom debate.	Conduct a mock trial after reading *To Kill a Mockingbird.*	Students develop a problem that interests them; have them work together in groups in a laboratory setting to create and to carryout experiments relevant to their chosen problem.
Intrapersonal (the intelligence of self-knowledge)	Interview an expert in the field of mathematics to explore long-term career goals.	After attending a career fair, write about a career of interest.	Each student pretends to be a famous person in a situation that the class has studied. Have each student write or discuss how he/she might have approached the situation differently.	Students discuss how science impacts them personally and what lifestyle changes, if any, they should make as a result.
Naturalist (the surrounding nature)	Students identify ways in which mathematicians can assist biologists and geologists with their work.	Write about out-door education opportunities (develop a play, fable, myth, short story) about the environment.	Students write or discuss how physical geography (land, water, animals, and plants) has affected the political development of a given country.	Visit zoos, nature parks, green houses, botanical gardens, and other outdoor environments; have students write about the experience.

Learning Styles

A discussion of learning styles should begin by answering the question, what is a learning style? Although Stahl (1999) argues against the existence of learning styles for academic subjects, and Berninger and Richards (2002) disaffirm learning styles for sensory modalities (e.g., visual, auditory, kinesthetic, tactile) or cerebral hemisphere (left brain–right brain), a sizable body of research suggests that learning styles theory is worth examining. Returning to the question at hand, what is a learning style? Silver, Strong, and Perini (2000) define learning styles as descriptions through which "we can talk about the way individuals learn and how their preferences for types of thinking processes affect their learning behaviors" (p. 24).

The Development of Learning Styles Theory

From the research of Dunn, Beaudry, and Klavas (1989), learning styles research has been classified into two categories: correlational and experimental. *Correlational* studies (Bruno, 1988; Cody, 1983) investigate the connections between individual preferences and other factors such as cognitive development, special learning abilities, and race; whereas *experimental* studies investigate the effects of learning style on achievement and attitude.

To provide some structure to the study of learning styles, models have been developed to explain learning differences in students. Because learning styles are unique to each individual, learning styles models are usually built around learning style inventories. For purposes of discussion, details of four models are presented here.

Models of Learning Styles

Learning styles theory traces its beginning with Carl Jung's (1927) *The Theory of Psychological Type,* in which Jung identifies four dimensions of personality:

> *sensation* tells you that something exists; *thinking* tells you what it is; *feeling* tells you whether it is agreeable or not; and *intuition* tells you from whence is comes and where it is going. (p. 481, emphasis in the original)

Jung's work provides the basis for several models. Silver, Strong, and Perini (1997) summarize learning styles research as having two commonalities "namely, a focus on process and an emphasis on personality" (p. 22).

Kolb's Theory of Experiential Learning

Kolb's (1984) model identifies four learning styles based on two continua: one depicting perceptive preferences (from concrete to abstract); and the other, cognitive processing preferences (from experimentation to reflection). The four learning styles are listed here:

1. *Accommodators* (concrete experience/active experimenter) who thrive on independent discovery and who prefer to be active learners

2. *Assimilators* (abstract conceptualization/reflective observer) who prefer organized delivery of content and who are most naturally passive learners

3. *Convergers* (abstract conceptualization/active experimenter) who like interactive learning and who want to discover how things work

4. *Divergers* (concrete experience/reflective observers) are similar to assimilators, but divergers want to explore why.

Silver and Hanson's Four Learning Styles Model

Silver and Hanson (1998) developed a model comprising four learning styles based on Jung's work.

1. *Mastery style,* which combines sensation and thinking. The mastery learner is realistic, practical, and results oriented.

2. *Understanding style,* which combines intuition and thinking. The understanding learner is theoretical and knowledge oriented.

3. *Interpersonal style,* which combines sensation and feeling. The interpersonal learner is sociable, sensitive, and interpersonally oriented.

4. *Self-expressive style,* which combines intuition and feeling. The self-expressive learner is curious, insightful, imaginative, and dares to dream. (pp. 58–59)

Dunn and Dunn's Model of Learning Styles

First developed in 1967, the Dunn and Dunn (1978) model of learning styles is grounded in cognitive style theory and brain lateralization theory. Cognitive styles theory is rooted in the belief that learners process information differently on the basis of inherited or learned traits. Brain lateralization theory states that the two hemispheres of the brain have different functions. The Dunn and Dunn model includes 21 elements organized into five strands to describe a person's learning preferences. Figure 5.3 depicts Dunn and Dunn's 21 elements of learning style.

Figure 5.3. Dunn and Dunn's 21 Elements of Learning Styles

Strand	*Elements*
Environmental	Sound, light, temperature, design
Emotional	Motivation, persistence, responsibility, structure
Sociological	Self, pair, peers, team, adult, varied
Physiological	Perceptual, intake, time, mobility
Psychological	Global/analytic, hemisphericity, impulsive/reflective

Keefe's Learning Styles

Keefe (1987) identifies learning styles based on preferences and skills classified into three major categories: cognitive styles, affective styles, and physiological styles. Cognitive styles are subdivided into reception styles (how a student perceives and receives new information) and concept formation and retention styles (how quickly and in what way a person organizes information). Affective learning styles include attention styles (conditions most conducive for a student's ability to focus attention) and expectancy and incentive styles (how fully a student accepts responsibility for his or her learning). Physiological styles include factors such as gender, overall health, preferred time of day to learn, the student's need for changes in body posture, and environmental elements such as light and temperature.

Learning styles are as individual as fingerprints (Dunn, Beaudry, & Klavas, 1989). Although two models (Kolb, 1984; Silver & Hanson, 1998) each describe four general learning styles, the remaining models (Dunn & Dunn, 1978; Keefe, 1987) provides a list of elements from which many different learning styles can be devised. The assertion begs the question, how does a teacher tailor instruction to address a classroom full of individual learners? The answer lies in the idea of differentiated instruction.

Using Brain Research, Multiple Intelligences, and Learning Styles to Differentiate Instruction

Brain research, the theory of multiple intelligences, and models of learning styles all suggest the need for instruction that is customized for the learners. Tomlinson (1999) refers to this way of teaching as differentiated instruction, and she provides numerous suggestions:

- *The teacher focuses on the essentials.* Because the brain is structured so that we forget more than we can remember, it is crucial for teachers to articulate what is essential for learners to be able to recall.

Adapted from Keefe (1987) *Learning Style: Theory and Practice.* Reston, VA: National Association of Secondary School Principals.

- *The teacher attends to student differences.* Students do not quest for sameness, but for the sense of triumph when they are respected, valued, nurtured, and even cajoled into accomplishing things they believe are beyond their grasp.

- *Assessment and instruction are inseparable.* In a differentiated classroom, assessment is ongoing and diagnostic and provides teachers with day-to-day data on students' readiness for learning.

- *The teacher modifies content, process, and products.* By thoughtfully using assessment data, the teacher can modify content (what she wants students to learn), process (activities designed to ensure that students make sense out of essential information), and product (vehicles through which students demonstrate and extend what they have learned).

- *All students participate in respectful work.* In differentiated classrooms, teachers continually try to understand what individual students need to learn by honoring both their commonalities and their differences, not by treating them alike.

- *The teacher and students collaborate in learning.* Teachers are the chief architects of learning, but students should assist with the design and building.

- *The teacher balances group and individual norms.* In an effectively differentiated classroom, assessment, instruction, feedback, and grading take into account both group and individual norms.

- *The teacher and students work together flexibly.* The teacher draws on a wide range of instructional strategies that help her focus on individuals and small groups, not just the whole class. (pp. 9–13)

Because teaching is composed of the delivery of instruction and assessment, ways to differentiate each of these components will be examined separately.

Differentiating the delivery of instruction requires teachers to become proficient in the use of multiple teaching strategies. Instructional decisions are based on the knowledge a teacher has about their students and empirically based research (e.g., brain research, multiple intelligences, learning styles). Figure 5.4 illustrates the intersections among select instructional strategies and brain research, multiple intelligences, and learning styles.

Figure 5.4. Intersections Among Instruction and Brain Research, Multiple Intelligences, and Learning Styles

Method	Applications to Brain Research	Multiple Intelligences Addressed	Sample Compatible Learning Styles and Preferences
Cooperative Learning	Wolfe & Brandt's emotion and learning Berninger & Richards's enriched environment	Interpersonal intelligence	Dunn & Dunn's sociological factors Kolb's divergers Silver & Hanson's interpersonal style
Direct Instruction (Lecture)	Supports short-term memory	Interpersonal intelligence Intrapersonal intelligence	Dunn & Dunn's emotional structure factor and physiological intake factor Kolb's assimilators Silver & Hanson's mastery style
Discussion	Berninger & Richards's enriched environment	Interpersonal intelligence Verbal intelligence	Dunn & Dunn's environmental sound and physiological intake Kolb's assimilators Silver & Hanson's interpersonal style
Inquiry	Ramey & Ramey's theory of brain plasticity	Spatial intelligence	Keefe's curiosity attention style Kolb's accommodators Silver & Hanson's self-expressive style
Simulations	Wolfe's (2001) performance for long-term memory	Can involve all of Gardner's intelligences	Keefe's conceptual vs. perceptual cognitive style Kolb's convergers Silver & Hanson's self-expressive style

Equally important to the delivery of instruction is the assessment of student learning. Teachers who differentiate their instructional practices need to use multiple assessment techniques. Figure 5.6 illustrates applications of various assessment techniques to differentiated instruction.

**Figure 5.5. Applications of Assessment Techniques
to Match Differentiated Instruction**

Method	Brain Research	Multiple Intelligences	Learning Styles/ Elements Addressed
Objective Tests	Coding into short-term memory	Linguistic intelligence Mathematical intelligence	Dunn & Dunn's environmental factorsKeefe's cognitive automazation and affective level of anxiety Kolb's assimilators Silver & Hanson's understanding style
Performances (speeches, simulations)	Requires "working memory" (Baddeley, 1986) D'Arcangelo's enriched learning environment	All intelligences can be addressed	Dunn & Dunn's emotional factors Keefe's concept leveling/sharpening Kolb's divergers Silver & Hanson's self-expressive style
Essays	Berninger & Richards's short- and long-term memory	Linguistic Intelligence	Dunn & Dunn's sociological self and psychological hemisphericity Keefe's conceptualizing styles Kolb's assimilators Silver & Hanson's self-expressive style
Portfolio Development	Berninger & Richards's brain plasticity	Spatial intelligence Intrapersonal intelligence	Dunn & Dunn's psychological factors Keefe's cognitive scanning and affective self-actualizing style Kolb's accommodators Silver & Hanson's mastery style
Projects (e.g., dioramas)	Ramey & Ramey's development of intelligence	Spatial intelligence Musical intelligence Kinesthetic intelligence	Dunn & Dunn's sociological factors (self, team) and physiological mobility style Keefe's affective level of aspiration style and physiological mobility style Kolb's convergers Silver & Hanson's self-expressive style

Supervision to Support the Use of Brain Research, Multiple Intelligences, and Learning Styles

Data collected during classroom observations tend to describe teacher and student behaviors using a series of snapshots, with each piece of data depicting an isolated event occurring during a teaching episode. It is the aggregation and analysis of the data that permit the teacher and the supervisor to identify patterns through which a holistic image of teaching can be created. There are many classroom observation tools that can be used to collect data about teaching (Acheson & Gall, 2002; Zepeda, 2003b). Figure 5.6 describes applications of these tools to collect data about instruction. The key for success is for the supervisor to not only observe the teacher but also to observe students. Effective observation involves keeping one eye on the teacher and the other on the students, tracking the effect of teaching behaviors on student-behavior learning.

Figure 5.6. Application of Data Collection Techniques

Data Collection Techniques*	Information Tracked	Applications to Supervising Differentiated Instruction
On-task	Identifying which students are engaged in learning	Are all students engaged in meaningful work that respects their differences?
Verbal Flow	Identifying which students are engaged	Is the teacher focusing on the essentials? Is the teacher engaged in ongoing assessment of student learning?
Class Traffic	Identifying which students are interacting with the teacher and how often by mapping the teacher's position at different points during the teaching episode	Is the teacher giving evidence of attending to student differences? Are the students and teacher collaborating in learning?
Interaction Analysis	Identifies communication patterns and the types of communication occurring	Is the teacher focusing on the essentials? Is the teacher engaged in ongoing assessment of student learning?
Global Scan	Tracks which teaching strategies the teacher is using	Is the teacher balancing group and individual norms? Are the students and teacher working together flexibly?

* Adapted from Acheson & Gall, 2002; Zepeda, 2003a.

Narrow lens techniques (e.g., on-task, verbal flow, class traffic, interaction analysis) can help the supervisor and teacher to identify which students are engaged in learning and which are not. Global scan is a useful technique for tracking teaching methods used and general events in the classroom that can affect which students become engaged in learning. Combined with knowledge of each student's learning styles, the supervisor and teacher can make informed decisions on what instructional strategies and assessment techniques might encourage the nonparticipating students to become more involved in learning.

The core activity of any school is instruction. In today's atmosphere of increased levels of federally mandated testing, the stakes are higher than ever. Therefore, it is of critical importance to use every tool available to help teachers to plan and deliver instruction that addresses differentiated learners. Knowledge of brain research, multiple intelligences, and different learning styles can help teachers and supervisors in identifying ways to increase the engagement of each student in learning. Chapter 2 provided a more in depth discussion of tools that can assist supervisors in supporting teachers' efforts to differentiate instruction. Chapters 7 through 10 detail instruction and supervision across the content areas of mathematics, language arts/reading, social studies, and science at the elementary, middle, and high school. Chapter 6 examines the characteristics of learners at the elementary, middle, and high school levels to help the supervisor understand how students learn and as a way to inform discussions with teachers about differentiating instruction.

Suggested Readings

Benjamin, A. (2002). *Differentiated instruction: A guide for middle and high school teachers.* Larchmont, NY: Eye On Education.

Berninger, V. W., & Richards, T. L. (2002). *Brain literacy for educators and psychologists.* Amsterdam: Academic Press.

Dunn, R., & Dunn, K. (1978). *Teaching students through their individual learning styles: A practical approach.* Reston, VA: Reston Publishing Company.

Fogerty, R. (2002). *Brain compatible classrooms.* Arlington Heights, IL: Skylight Professional Development.

Gardner, H. (1993). *Frames of mind: The theory of multiple intelligences.* New York: Basic Books.

Gardner, H. (1999). *Intelligence reframed: Multiple intelligences for the 21st Century.* New York: Basic Books.

Parry, T., & Gregory, G. (2003). *Designing brain compatible learning* (2nd ed.). Glenview, IL: Skylight Professional Development.

Tomlinson, C. A. (1999). *The differentiated classroom: Responding to the needs of all learners.* Alexandria, VA: Association for Supervision and Curriculum Development.

6

Students as Learners

In this Chapter...

♦ Theories of psychological, social, and emotional development

♦ Elementary school learners

♦ Learners in middle schools

♦ High school learners

♦ Stages of development: Connections to the supervision of teachers

The purpose of supervision is the improvement of instruction and the development of the teacher (Blumberg, 1980; Cogan, 1973). To improve instruction, supervisors and teachers need relevant, stable observation data on which to base an ongoing plan for teacher learning. If observational data are to be meaningful, the supervisor first needs an understanding of what will be observed (Zepeda, 2003b). Making sense of classroom events requires an understanding of what is being taught, what methods are being used, and, perhaps most important, knowledge of the learners in the classroom.

Principals typically have responsibility for students across several grade levels, who are normally grouped based on homogeneity of psychological, social, and emotional development. Understanding the needs of learners can be difficult for the principal with limited experience at one grade level, as in the case of a principal new to an elementary school after serving as a high school assistant principal. Understanding how developmental factors affect learning can assist the principal in supporting teachers' efforts at making informed decisions about teaching and learning.

In this chapter, basic theories about psychological, social, and emotional development are presented and then discussed against the backdrops of elementary, middle, and high schools. Finally, connections between developmental stages of learners and the principal as supervisor are discussed.

Theories of Psychological, Social, and Emotional Development

Berk (2002) asserts much of what is known about the development of learning is based on the work of Jean Piaget (cognitive development theory), Erik Erikson (psychosocial development theory), and Albert Bandura (social learning theory). Four broad stages of cognitive development compose the foundation of Piaget's work.

Erikson's (1997) theory posits eight stages of psychological development theory, which describe interpersonal relationships and conflicts characteristic of each stage. The work of Bandura (1977) established the importance of modeling as a basis for children's learning.

Although some researchers question whether human cognitive development can be adequately portrayed by a stage model (Ormrod, 2000), perhaps the most widely recognized model of cognitive development is that of Jean Piaget. Piaget's theory is based on the idea that children build cognitive structures, referred to as *mental maps*, or interrelated concepts, for understanding and responding to physical experiences within the environment. As children develop, according to Piaget's theory, their cognitive structures and reasoning abilities increase to highly complex mental activities. Composed of four stages, Piaget's (1977) theory depicts human cognitive development from birth through adulthood. The four stages are briefly described in Figure 6.1.

Figure 6.1. Piaget's Stages of Cognitive Development

Stage	Approximate Age Range	Characteristics
Sensorimotor Stage	Birth to 2 years	Infants are incapable of mental processes concerning objects they cannot see partly because of a lack of language development.
Preoperational Stage	2 years to 6 or 7 years	Young children are capable of mental processes concerning objects they cannot see, but they do not have developed logical thinking skills.
Concrete Operational Stage	6 or 7 years to 11 or 12 years	Older children and young adolescents have developed logical thinking skills, but these skills are limited to concrete reality.
Formal Operational Stage	11 or 12 years to adulthood	Older adolescents and adults can extend logical reasoning to abstract concepts.

Source: Adapted from Ormrod (2000), *Educational Psychology: Developing Learners*, 3rd Edition and Piaget (1952), *The origins of intelligence in children.*

Understanding the cognitive developmental levels of learners is essential to develop an effective instructional program. Regardless of grade level, a developmentally appropriate curriculum and equally developmentally appropriate instructional strategies need to be used to enhance student logical and conceptual growth needs. The intent of instruction should be to assist learners in building cognitive structures. Whereas early primary and elementary educators serve learners best with instruction that emphasizes experience through interaction with others and their immediate surroundings to build logical thinking skills, middle-level educators need to reinforce concrete thinking skills and to support the acquisition of abstract thinking. Principals and teachers in high schools need to plan instruction that supports learners' extension of abstract thinking skills.

Erikson (1997) theorized eight levels of psychological development. Figure 6.2 (page 110) summarizes these stages.

Teachers and principals in the elementary arena need to develop instructional programs that allow students to discover their strengths in a nonthreatening environment. The elementary school experience provides an important foundation for how students perceive the school experience. As learners transition to the middle school and high school, the investigation of who they are and how they fit into the scheme of things continues. Broderick and Blewitt (2003) assert that elementary school and middle school students need to learn important academic skills and how to view themselves as comparing favorably with their peers, whereas high school students need support as they begin making decision about values and vocations.

Social learning theory asserts that many people learn by watching others and determining which behaviors result in positive reinforcement and which result in negative reinforcement (Berk, 2002; Ormrod, 2000). One of the most important of the social learning theorists, Bandura (1977) proposed that important learning occurs through observation and modeling, and he identified five functions included in this type of learning: attention, coding, retaining, carrying out motor functions, and motivation (pp. 22–29).

When learning through modeling, the learner, according to Bandura, must first *attend* to the relevant information gained from the stimulus while filtering out irrelevant information. Second, the learner *codes* by assigning a visual image or a semantic code to relevant information to facilitate recall. A third factor in learning through modeling is *retaining* information. Bandura (1969) believed that retention is a major difficulty for children. Too often, information needed to solve problems is not accessible. *Carrying out motor functions* occurs when the learner forms an action plan and then carries out that plan. Finally, for any of the first four functions to occur, the learner must be *motivated*.

Figure 6.2. Erikson's Eight Levels of Psychosocial Development

Stage	Approximate Age Range	Description
Trust vs. Mistrust	Birth to 1 year	Without basic trust, the infant cannot survive. With trust comes the strength of hope (p. 106).
Autonomy vs. Shame & Doubt	1 to 3 years	Toddlers display the will to do new things. Overstepping limits can lead to insecurity and a lack of self-confidence. Shame and doubt in their capacities can result (p. 107).
Initiative vs. Guilt	3 to 6 years	Preschool children begin exploring often involving role playing. Initiation is valiant, but when it misfires, a strong sense of deflation and guilt can follow (p. 108).
Industry vs. Inferiority	6 to 12 years	School age children discover what they are good at and what they are good for. Negative experiences can lead to feelings of inferiority (p. 109).
Identity Role vs. Confusion	12 to 20 years	The greatest problem encountered is who we think we are versus who others may think we are or are trying to be (p. 110).
Intimacy vs. Isolation	Young Adulthood	To love and find oneself in another brings fulfillment and delight (p. 110).
Generativity vs. Stagnation	Middle Adulthood	This stage covers the longest stretch of life. In this stage one establishes a working commitment and perhaps begins a family (p. 111).
Ego Integrity vs. Despair	Late Adulthood	Lifetime of learning results in high level of integrity. Decline in ability because of aging can lead to despair (p. 112).

Source: Adapted from Erikson (1997), *The Life Cycle Completed.*

Elementary School Learners

As students enter formal schooling, they have just finished one of the fastest periods of development they will ever experience. The average 6-year-old is about 3.5 feet tall, weighs approximately 45 pounds (Butler, McKie, & Ratcliffe (1990), and has already developed a vocabulary of about 10,000 words (Berk, 2002). The beginning elementary school learner is just starting to develop basic logic skills (Piaget, 1952) and to discover what he or she does and does not do well (Erikson, 1997). During the elementary school years, children learn important social skills and memory skills, as well as academic skills (Broderick & Blewitt, 2003).

Elementary school children are capable of logical thinking skills about concrete objects with which they are familiar. Flavell, Miller, and Miller (1993) reported that children have a tendency to "hug the ground of empirical reality" (p. 139). When asked to think abstractly, elementary students normally attempt to find a concrete equivalent to use as a frame of reference (Broderick & Blewitt, 2003). Three major concrete operational skills develop during the elementary school years include conservation, classification, and seriation (Berk, 2002).

Ormrod (2000) defined *conservation* as the ability "to recognize that amount stays the same if nothing has been added or taken way, even if the substance is reshaped or rearranged" (p. 34). For example, if the contents of a tall, slender glass are poured into a short, shallow container, a child with conservation skills (Piaget's stage of concrete, operational thought) recognizes that the *amount* of water has not changed. A student who is still operating at the Piaget's preoperational stage believes that a change in shape does equal a change in amount. The ability to reverse the steps taken to solve a problem, called reversibility, also occurs as a part of the development of conservation skills (Piaget, 1977).

Classification refers to the awareness of two or more groups of related objects. Development of classification skills is evident in a child's collection of baseball cards, coins, or stamps (Berk, 2002). Educators support the development of classification skills through the use of manipulatives. For example, a student who sorts pictures of railroad cars by color, car type, or size is learning classification skills. Ormrod (2000) reports that as children advance in their classification skills, they exhibit advanced skills such as multiple classification (classification into two or more categories simultaneously) and deductive reasoning (drawing logical conclusions based on the facts available).

The ability to properly sequence objects by size is called *seriation.* Seriation can be learned by ordering a group of students by height or a collection of sticks by length. A related, though more advanced skill, is transitivity (Piaget, 1969). For example, if student A is taller than student B, and student B is taller than student C, then using transitivity, one can deduce that student A is taller than student C.

During the elementary school years, students' ability to store and to retrieve information progresses markedly. Memory strategies such as rehearsal, organization, and elaboration begin to occur (Berk, 2002). A student who repeats a list of presidents or the parts of speech to recall them for a test is using rehearsal. Organization refers to the grouping of related pieces of information for the purpose of memorizing them. For example, to learn the names of the presidents, a student might group presidents chronologically (begin by learning the first 10 presidents) or geographically (Gathercole, 1998). Broderick and Blewitt (2003) define elaboration as "finding or creating some kind of meaningful link between items" (p. 207) to remember them, and they report the use of elaboration becomes spontaneous by the beginning of middle school. Erikson (1997) reports as children reach elementary school age, they are beginning the transition from stage 3 (initiative versus guilt) to stage 4 (industry versus inferiority). Learners in the elementary grades have sufficient social and emotional development to begin working together. By the late elementary years (about grades 4 and 5), children develop a well-defined self-concept, and children are more likely to describe themselves in more objective terms (Harter, 1996).

Self-esteem is usually quite high for preschoolers. When students enter elementary school, self-esteem fluctuates based on the influence of tests, teacher comments, and even selection for activities in physical education classes—"I'm always picked last!" Elementary school students also have their first experiences with the self-conscious emotions of guilt and pride (Berk, 2002). Selman (1976) reported that children's abilities to understand another person's perspective increases. Socially, peer groups begin to form. Because of the self-contained nature of elementary school classrooms, the development of these peer groups is based on proximity. Students who share a common teacher are likely to be members of the same peer groups (Berk, 2002).

The Supervisor's Scorecard

Interaction and instruction are enhanced through

♦ Care for the self-esteem of the learners

♦ Modeling prosocial behaviors

♦ Inclusiveness for individuals

♦ Promoting self-expression and the sharing of ideas

♦ Cooperative models of instruction and experiential learning techniques

♦ Positive learning environments

Learners in Middle Schools

Perhaps no descriptor more accurately describes the middle-level learner than change. Identifying the changes experienced during early adolescence is only part of the battle, according to Knowles and Brown (2000):

> Creating a school environment that is responsive to the changing needs of young adolescents requires an understanding of their developmental changes. More important, however, it requires an understanding of how young adolescents perceive those changes. Their perceptions become their reality. (p. 8)

The changes experienced by middle-level learners occur at several levels. These changes include physical development, intellectual development, social development, and emotional development (George & Alexander, 1993).

A look inside any middle school or junior high school would reveal the diverse rates at which middle-level students develop physically. In many classrooms, teachers can find students who exhibit outward signs of physical and sexual maturity alongside those who have yet to experience the onset of puberty. Underlying the physical changes, hormones also can have profound effects on middle-level learners' behaviors (Broderick & Blewitt, 2003). However, the role of hormones by themselves on the behaviors of middle-level learners has been a source of some disagreement. Brooks-Gunn and Warren (1989) expressed doubt as to whether hormones alone could be held accountable for adolescents' changing behavior: "Even if hormonal effects are demonstrated, they must be evaluated relative to contextual effects and relative to interactive effects before assuming a direct relation between hormones and behavior" (p. 51).

For principals in middle schools, the importance of understanding the physical changes experienced by young adolescents is the connection between physical changes in other areas. Knowles and Brown (2000) report that "although

physical changes are the most obvious and visible of the changes [in early ado-
lescence], it is the impact of physical maturation on emotional and social development that has the greatest influence on how young adolescents view themselves" (p. 17), and how middle school children view themselves affects
learning.

Learners in middle schools attach great significance to their physical ap-
pearances. While young adolescents are struggling to understand the myriad
physical changes they are experiencing, they are also attempting to learn a new
way of thinking. Learners in middle schools find themselves at the cusp between Piaget's (1977) concrete operational and formal operational stages. In
practical terms, these learners are trying to build the bridge from concrete
thought to abstract thought. The emerging ability to think abstractly produces a
high level of inquisitiveness in middle-level learners. Instruction needs to capitalize on middle-level learners' natural inquisitiveness (Knowles & Brown,
2000):

> Middle school students are learners in the purest sense of the word.
> Based on a developing capacity for abstract thinking, middle school
> students are curious about life and highly inquisitive about every-
> thing life has to offer. They challenge principles that don't fit their
> view of the way things work. This curiosity leads to the desire to par-
> ticipate in practical problem solving and activities that reflect real is-
> sues. (pp. 20–21)

Middle school learners need to be active learners. Because of the variety of
developmental rates among middle-level learners, some students remain at the
concrete stage throughout their entire middle school tenure (Eson & Wolmsky,
1980).

Closely related to physical and cognitive development, the social development of middle-level learners also plays an important part in how young adolescents learn. The very structure of elementary schools and middle schools creates a major social transition for early adolescents. Knowles and Brown point
out that "at a time when dramatic physical and intellectual changes are occurring, children are taken from the safety and security of the self-contained elementary classroom and put into an alien environment" (p. 21). Because of the
structure of the middle school, students move from classroom to classroom
throughout the day, and they are required to learn the rules and regulations of
up to six or seven different teachers. The result of this new environment that
includes many new people and new structures for the early adolescent creates a
forced social change on top of the already confusing physical and cognitive
changes they are experiencing.

In the middle grades, students begin learning to identify different groups
within their schools. Because physical maturation is the yardstick by which

middle-level learners interpret their social status, physical development can exert considerable influence on their social development. George and Alexander argue that "development perceived by the student to be abnormal can cause great anxiety and influence social and emotional development" (p. 6). As a result, the formation of social groups may be affected. In addition, the influence of social groups on individual middle-level learners increases. An important social transition takes place during the middle school years as these learners begin exploring independence from their families for the first time (Knowles & Brown, 2000). During this time, middle-level learners also search for an individual identity.

Just as middle-level learners find themselves at a crossroads in cognitive development, so it is with their social and emotional development. In reviewing Erikson's (1997) stages of psychosocial development, it becomes clear that middle-level students are transitioning from stage 4 to stage 5, in which they move from learning how to work to together to learning who they are. Erikson compares this search for identity to role-playing:

> We play roles, of course, and try out parts we wish we could play for real, especially as we explore in adolescence. Costumes and makeup may sometimes be persuasive, but in the long run it is only having a genuine sense of who we are that keeps our feet on the ground and our heads up to an elevation from which we can see clearly where we are, what we are, and what we stand up for. (p. 110)

Middle-level learners experience a confusing array of changes. These changes encompass their physical, cognitive, social, and emotional development. However, early adolescents are eager and inquisitive learners who need to be taught across all levels: cognitive, social, and emotional. Principals and teachers need to provide an instructional program that addresses middle-level learners' needs, George and Alexander (1993) conclude that

> educators assume that such [social and emotional] skills are part of the implicit curriculum, in point of fact, that need to be *taught*. Defining the sense of self, independence, and changing relationships with others are areas that need to be explored within the school program. (pp. 13–14, emphasis in the original)

The Supervisor's Scorecard

For the middle-level learner, instruction should be varied to

♦ Promote inquisitiveness

♦ Capitalize on the physical need for movement

♦ Meet needs through developing meaningful relationships with teachers

♦ Attend to an attention span of approximately 10 minutes by using a variety of instructional strategies

♦ Help middle school children further develop their sense of self-esteem and promote a sense of belonging

♦ Scaffold instruction from "baby steps" to more complex applications of knowledge through such means as using thematic units where teachers across content areas teach and reinforce learning

---

High School Learners

Just as middle school learners were discussed against the backdrop of change, high school students could be described by the term *identity*. High school students begin the process of developing the identities they will take into adulthood: "What makes this particular period of the life cycle remarkable are the impressive strides young people make during the years of adolescence and young adulthood in developing the essential core of how they will be as adults" (Broderick & Blewitt, 2003, p. 331). Expanded opportunities in academics, athletics, academic and service clubs, and student government organizations support the physical, cognitive, social, and emotional development necessary to the formation of identity.

Although many students are physically mature by the time they enter high school, some are not. Late maturity can have profound effects on adolescents, especially males. Simmons and Blythe (1987) reported that late maturing adolescent males are more likely to experience awkwardness, insecurity, and moodiness. Although late physical maturation is less of an issue with girls, body image and weight can be major issues for high school girls (Mendelson, White, & Mendelson, 1996). As a result of continuing physical development, most adolescents who become sexually active do so about the time they enter high school (Rodgers, 1996).

Even as many adolescents are still developing physically as they begin high school, so is their cognitive development. Recent studies (Casey, Giedd, & Thomas, 2000; Sowell, Delis, Stiles, & Jernigan, 2001) indicate that many areas of the brain, including the frontal, parietal, and temporal lobes, are still developing. These areas of the brain affect emotions, information integration, and language skills. This continued physical development of the brain supports the continued evolvement of formal operational thought in older adolescents.

Piaget (1952) believed that adolescents transition from concrete operational thought to formal operational thought. However, this process is not lockstep among high school students (Ormrod, 2000). Individual adolescents may experience the development of formal operational thought at first in a single discipline, such as history or science, (Broderick & Blewitt, 2003) and then later in other areas. Although adolescents experience the transition to formal operational thought at different times, most make this transition during the high school years. Research suggests that the number of adolescents using formal operational thought doubles while in high school (Cowan, 1978; Gray, 1990).

During their high school years, adolescents begin developing other important cognitive tools. Metacognitive processes, the ability to form some understanding of one's own cognitive processes, is dependent on the development of formal operational thought. Broderick and Blewitt (2003) assert that "planful, organized thinking about one's own thought processes involves logical thinking about an abstraction—thought. The capacity for formal operational thinking seems to give this process a strong boost" (p. 328).

Three other major facets of the cognitive development of high school students bear mention: imaginary audience, personal fable, and invincibility fable (Elkind, 1984). High school students, in their struggle to build a more adult identity, sometimes believe that the world is watching them. This is referred to as the *imaginary audience*. The existence of an imaginary audience can fuel another facet of cognitive development, the *personal fable* in which adolescents develop a misshapen view of their own importance. The need to establish independence from family and the need to form an adult identity are strong contributors to the development of a personal fable (Lapsley, 1993).

Closely related to the personal fable, the *invincibility fable* influences some adolescents to believe they cannot be hurt, and some even begin to believe in their own immortality. Ormrod (2000) argues that the invincibility fable can help explain why high school students seem especially vulnerable to high-risk behaviors such as drug abuse, unprotected sexual activity, and unsafe driving habits.

Socially, high school students tend to identify themselves and each other in terms of group membership: athletic teams, clubs, and honor societies. These *peer* groups provide a source of support as adolescents begin exploring new levels of independence from their families (Broderick & Blewitt, 2003). Recent research (Barber, Eccles, & Stone, 2001; Steinberg, 1996) has identified commonly found peer groups in American high schools. These include popularity-oriented groups (about 20% of student enrollment), outsider groups (about 20%), and average groups (about 30%). Only about 5% aspire to high academic achievement. Peer influence, which actually peaks in middle school, has been identified as a major source of problem behaviors and academic underachievement that plagues some 10th through 12th graders (Fuligni, Eccles, Barber, & Clements, 2001).

Stages of Development: Connections to the Supervision of Teachers

Knowledge of learners' cognitive, social, and emotional development can help principals in making informed judgments based on data collected during classroom observations. These data represent two types of behaviors: teacher behaviors and student behaviors. Student behaviors tend to depend on following teachers' instructions and imitating skills modeled by teachers. Central issues include the selection of teaching developmentally appropriate instructional strategies, selection of materials and equipment to assist in the delivery of instruction, and the use of content that is relevant and interesting to students. The critical question that comes to mind is, "What teacher or student behaviors would signal developmental appropriateness to the principal?"

At the elementary level, many teachers use manipulatives to help students learn skills such as sequencing, counting, and classification. Because these learners, especially in the early grades, are operating at Piaget's preoperational stage, their ability to think logically about objects they cannot see is, at best, primitive. Additionally, elementary teachers tend to transition to new learning activities often. As children mature, they are capable of higher levels of thought over more sustained periods of time.

Children in the middle schools have more developed logical skills and are capable of more complex thought. Because of the myriad physical changes taking place, middle school students still need to change activities fairly often. As these students transition to high school, they develop the ability to think abstractly. It is natural that more complex tasks such as analysis of literature, advanced mathematical problem solving, and scientific reasoning become standard activities in the classroom.

In addition to appropriate content and tasks, appropriate teaching strategies are needed. Use of lecture should probably be limited in the elementary arena because of the limited attention span and lack of abstract thinking skills in young children. Hands-on teaching strategies such as inquiry are appropriate. Complex strategies such as Socratic Seminars (see Chapter 4) and some simulations are also more appropriate at the middle or high school level.

Principals observe teachers to collect data about teacher behaviors and student behaviors. From these data, growth plans are developed, staff development activities may be planned, and changes in teaching practices may be made. At year end, these data are customarily incorporated into a rating assigned by the principal. Because of the myriad important uses of the data collected during classroom observations, the importance of understanding of the learners' cognitive, social, and emotional stages emerges.

The Supervisor's Scorecard

For the supervisor, it is important to be able to give feedback to teachers about

- their engagement of the learner through the content;

- their instructional methods used to deliver the content;

- the types of activities the learners are engaged in;

- the resources used to enhance learning experiences;

- the types of assessments used to support judgments about learning.

The supervisor should consult Chapter 2 and Figure 2.3, the Pre-observation Conference Form, especially the section on the classroom environment (presented in Figure 6.3)

Figure 6.3. The Classroom Environment

Schools are diverse. It is not likely that every math teacher who teaches Algebra I teaches it the same. This part of the pre-observation form focuses on the characteristics, culture, and climate of the classroom-learning environment.

Characteristics of the Learner. What are students like? Are students on an even playing field in relation to performance, motivational levels, and abilities? Are there students with special learning needs that require modification to instruction and assessment of learning?

Culture and Climate. How would you characterize the atmosphere in the room? Probe teachers to talk about "how things are run," "the roles students assume in the learning process," "the way students communicate with one another and you," "the levels of cooperation," "student attitudes," and "student behavior and hot spots."

Source: Zepeda (2003b).

The more the supervisor understands about the learners in a particular classroom and the instructional objectives for the lesson, the more focused the observation will be. The next few chapters examine supervision across the content areas of mathematics, English/language arts, social studies, and science.

Suggested Readings

Berk, L. A. (2002). *Infants, children, and adolescents* (4th ed.). Boston: Allyn & Bacon.

Broderick, P. C., & Blewitt, P. (2003). *The life span: Human development for helping professionals.* Upper Saddle River, NJ: Merrill Prentice Hall.

Charlesworth, R. (2004). *Understanding child development* (6th ed.). Clifton Park, NY: Thomson Learning.

Erikson, E. H. (1997). *The life cycle completed.* New York: Norton.

Gathercole, S. E. (1998). The development of memory. *Journal of Child Psychology and Psychiatry, 39*(1), 3–27.

Piaget, J. (1977). *The development of thought: Elaboration of cognitive structures.* New York: Viking.

7

Supervision in the Mathematics Classroom

In this Chapter...

♦ Standards for mathematics instruction

♦ Mathematics content across the PreK–12 continuum

♦ Mathematics and human development theory—implications for instruction

♦ Instructional strategies for mathematics learning

♦ The supervisor in the mathematics classroom

On October 4, 1957, the Soviet Union launched *Sputnik I,* the first man-made satellite in space. Believing that an educational emergency existed, the United States Congress passed the National Defense Education Act of 1958, infusing millions of federal dollars to overhaul mathematics, science, and foreign language instruction in America's public schools. As a result, multiple strategies for organizing and delivering mathematics instruction were published.

Over the past 40 years, mathematics has been one of the most often mentioned sore spots in public education. Ingersoll (1995) reports that mathematics is the subject with the highest percentage of out-of-field teachers. The National Center for Education Statistics (1996) indicates that "of all teachers who teach at least one high school mathematics class... almost one-third did not have a college major or minor in mathematics or mathematics education" (p. 1). What can be gleaned from Ingersoll and the NCES report on underqualified and out-of-field teachers teaching mathematics? Teachers who do not have a deep understanding of content and facility with teaching mathematics need more assistance, whether this assistance comes from a supervisor during and after a classroom observation or from a peer coach or a mentor.

Supervising instruction for the principal not trained in mathematics can cause increased levels of anxiety when confronted with the task of supervising mathematics teachers. Yet, as a core area of the curriculum across the PreK–12 curriculum, the stakes are high for supervisors who do not have a basic understanding of instruction in mathematics and the knowledge to help teachers improve their teaching.

The purposes of this chapter are to acquaint principals with the standards for mathematics instruction, introduce them to appropriate instructional strategies for teaching mathematics at all levels, and offer strategies for supervising in the mathematics classroom.

Standards for Mathematics Instruction

Standards for the instruction of mathematics are written and published by the National Council of Teachers of Mathematics (NCTM). Standards are listed with the permission of the National Council of Teachers of Mathematics (NCTM). NCTM does not endorse the content or validity of these alignments. NCTM defines one set of standards for all students grades PreK–12. The NCTM Standards are defined in terms of 10 broad areas. Figure 7.1 lists these standards.

Figure 7.1. NCTM Standards[1]

Standard	NCTM Content Standards
Number and Operations Standard	Instructional programs from prekindergarten through grade 12 should enable all students to—understand numbers, ways of representing numbers, relationships among numbers and number systems; understand meanings of operations and how they relate to one another; compute fluently and make reasonable estimates.
Algebra Standard	Instructional programs from prekindergarten through grade 12 should enable all students to—understand patterns, relations, and functions; represent and analyze mathematical situations and structures using algebraic symbols; use mathematical models to represent and understand quantitative relationships; analyze changes in various contexts.

---

1   Standards are listed with the permission of the National Council of Teachers of Mathematics (NCTM). NCTM does not endorse the content or validity of these alignments.

Standard	*NCTM Content Standards*
Number and Operations Standard	Instructional programs from prekindergarten through grade 12 should enable all students to—understand numbers, ways of representing numbers, relationships among numbers and number systems; understand meanings of operations and how they relate to one another; compute fluently and make reasonable estimates.
Geometry Standard	Instructional programs from prekindergarten through grade 12 should enable all students to—analyze characteristics and properties of two- and three-dimensional geometric shapes and develop mathematical arguments about geometric relationships; specify locations and describe spatial relationships using coordinate geometry and other representational systems; apply t ransformations and use symmetry to analyze mathematical situations; use visualization, spatial reasoning, and geometric modeling to solve problems.
Measurement Standard	Instructional programs from prekindergarten through grade 12 should enable all students to—understand measurable attributes of objects and the units, systems, and processes of measurement; apply appropriate techniques, tools, and formulas to determine measurement.
Problem Solving Standard	Instructional programs from prekindergarten through grade 12 should enable all students to—build new mathematical knowledge through problem solving; solve problems that arise in mathematics and other contexts; apply and adapt a variety of appropriate strategies to solve problems; monitor and reflect on the process of mathematical problem solving.
Reasoning and Proof Standard	Instructional programs from prekindergarten through grade 12 should enable all students to—recognize reasoning and proof and fundamental aspects of mathematics; make and investigate mathematical conjectures; develop and evaluate mathematical arguments and proofs; select and use various types of reasoning and methods of proof.
Communication Standard	Instructional programs from prekindergarten through grade 12 should enable all students to—organize and consolidate their mathematical thinking through communication; communicate their mathematical thinking coherently and clearly to peers, teachers, and others; analyze and evaluate the mathematics thinking and strategies of others; use the language of mathematics to express mathematical ideas precisely.
Connections Standard	Instructional programs from prekindergarten through grade 12 should enable all students to—recognize and use connections among mathematical ideas; understand how mathematical ideas interconnect and build on one another to produce a coherent whole; recognize and apply mathematics in contexts outside of mathematics.

Standard	NCTM Content Standards
Number and Operations Standard	Instructional programs from prekindergarten through grade 12 should enable all students to—understand numbers, ways of representing numbers, relationships among numbers and number systems; understand meanings of operations and how they relate to one another; compute fluently and make reasonable estimates.
Representation Standard	Instructional programs from prekindergarten through grade 12 should enable all students to—create and use representations to organize, record, and communicate mathematical ideas; select, apply, and translate among mathematical representations to solve problems; use representations to model and interpret physical, social, and mathematical phenomena.

Specific expectations for how the standards should be met are offered for four grade groupings: PreK–2, 3–5, 6–8, and 9–12. The following section examines the NCTM Standards relative to math instruction.

NCTM Standards for Grades PreK–2

Much of the mathematics learning that occurs during the early school years is reflected in a child's routine activities. The National Council of Teachers of Mathematics (2000b) asserts that children

> learn mathematical concepts through everyday activities: sorting (putting toys or groceries away), reasoning (comparing and building with blocks), representing (drawing to record ideas), recognizing patterns (talking about daily routines, repeating nursery rhymes, and reading predictable books), following directions (singing motion songs), and using spatial visualization (working puzzles). Using objects, role-playing, drawing ,and counting, children show what they know. (p. 74)

The NCTM Standards for the early grades emphasize the basic skills of counting, sorting, comparing, matching, taking things apart, and putting things together. The NCTM also recommends using technology such as simple calculators in the early grades, but cautions teachers that students need to learn when calculator use is appropriate and when it is not.

Numbers and operations standards for the early grades emphasize addition and subtraction, whole numbers, and the recognition of equal groupings (e.g., four groups of three objects each). This skill sets the foundation for future study of multiplication and division. Algebra standards require sorting, classifying, and ordering skills, along with knowledge of the commutative property of addition.

The geometry standards for the early grades include recognizing, drawing, and comparing shapes such as squares, circles, and triangles. Students in the early grades should also be able to demonstrate familiarity with terms such as *distance, direction,* and *near to.* These students, according to the measurement standards, should be able to sort objects by length, weight, and volume. Students in PreK–2 should also be able to describe weight, area, and time. Application of these skills includes the ability to measure length using objects such as erasers or paper clips. NCTM Standards at the PreK–2 level also expect students to learn basic problem solving skills. Here, problem solving is defined as a process comprised of three steps: understanding a problem, identifying possible strategies to resolve the problem, and determining which strategy or strategies were successful.

NCTM Standards for Grades 3–5

The NCTM Standards for grades 3–5 address the same categories as the PreK–2 standards. However, three new themes are introduced: multiplicative reasoning, equivalence, and computational fluency. Multiplicative reasoning is the ability to recognize when multiplication and division are appropriate tools and the ability to use these tools in solving problems. Equivalence refers to the ability to recognize different names for the same number (e.g., ¾ and .75). Computational fluency is defined as the ability to recognize and to use general rules called algorithms to solve mathematical problems.

According to the NCTM (2000b), it is during the upper elementary grades (3–5) that algebraic ideas begin to emerge and that the accompanying curiosity should be encouraged and nurtured. New concepts such as the associative property and the distributive property should be investigated. Students at this age should begin using letters such as x or y to represent unknown numbers. In geometry, students in grades 3–5 should be able to extend their work to three dimensional figures and use coordinate systems, especially to calculate distances between two points on horizontal or vertical axes (number lines).

Measurement standards for grades 3–5 require students to extend their knowledge of measurement to measuring angles and calculating simple conversions from one unit of measure to another (e.g., from feet to inches). Other new concepts at this level include perimeter, area, and volume. Students in grades 3–5 should also be expanding their knowledge of data analysis and probability. NCTM Standards expect these students to begin learning how specific questions can affect how data are collected and what measures such as mean and median can or cannot indicate about data. Additional skills described in the standards for grades 3–5 include learning the significance of counterexamples (examples that disprove a conjecture) and learning to solve problems in groups.

NCTM Standards for Grades 6–8

According to the NCTM (2000b), middle school is an important time in the mathematical development of students. It is during the middle school years that many students solidify their attitudes toward studying mathematics. The NCTM Standards for grades 6–8 recommend significant amounts of instruction in both algebra and geometry. Because much crucial development can take place in students during middle school, the NCTM Standards recommend strong professional development for middle-level mathematics teachers.

Students in the middle grades should be able to extend their problem-solving skills with fractions and decimals as well as their understanding of ratio and proportion (e.g., $1:2 = 2:x$; since $1 \times 2 = 2$, multiply 2×2 to discover that $x = 4$). Middle school students should also demonstrate the ability to use exponential (e.g., $2 \times 2 \times 2 = 2^3$) and scientific notations (e.g., $.00024 = 2.4 \times 10^{-4}$). Algebra standards for grades 6–8 expect students to increase their knowledge in the uses of variables and to extend the understanding of equations as representations of lines. For example, students seeing an equation such as $y = 3x + 4$ should recognize that this equation represents a line with a slope of 3 and that intersects the y-axis at the point (0,4).

In geometry, middle school students should begin learning to formulate inductive and deductive arguments, to use coordinate geometry to investigate polygons, to demonstrate understanding of congruence and similarity. Other new concepts for middle-level students include circles, trapezoids, prisms, pyramids, and velocity. Data analysis standards for grade 6–8 students are also extended. New concepts include populations and samples. These students are also expected to be able to analyze graphic depictions of data such as histograms, box plots, scatterplots, and stem-and-leaf plots.

NCTM Standards for Grades 9–12

The NCTM Standards for grades 9–12 assume that students will study mathematics during all four of their high school years. It is no surprise that the NCTM prescribes a rigorous high school mathematics curriculum designed to extend students' abilities to formulate formal mathematical arguments and to provide students with a strong conceptual foundation in the study of functions. The grades 9–12 standards also push for mathematics instruction that emphasizes depth over breadth and incorporates all appropriate technology. Mathematics curricula can create a quandary for mathematics teachers. There is usually more content required than can be easily accommodated in the time allotted most PreK–12 public school mathematics classrooms. The mathematics teacher is asked to make difficult decisions about which topics are given priority and which are not. The NCTM asserts that spending more time teaching fewer topics (teaching for depth) rather than teaching more topics in less time (teaching for breadth) will result in increased student learning.

Specific new topics in operations and number theory include learning about very large and very small numbers, how they are written (e.g., scientific notation), and when they are used; properties of number systems (e.g., real numbers, rational numbers); powers and roots; and how to manipulate vectors and matrices. Algebra standards are centered on developing knowledge of exponential, polynomial, rational, logarithmic, and periodic functions. Inequalities are also introduced. New topics in geometry include graphing using polar coordinates and developing the ability to write and critique formal proofs.

Mathematics Content Across the PreK–12 Continuum

Mathematics content across the PreK–12 continuum is, by nature, sequential. Although the content of PreK–12 mathematics curriculum may seem complex at first, a careful analysis reveals two major skills inherent in all mathematics classes: computation and application. For the purposes of this discussion, computation is defined as manipulation of numbers, for example addition and subtraction. Application refers to the ability to use computational skills to solve real-world problems. For example, students may be asked to determine how many apples could be purchased if apples cost 11¢ each and the purchaser has $1.43.

A review of the NCTM Standards reveals that these two skills are expected to permeate mathematics instruction at all levels in elementary, middle, and high school. With knowledge about computation and application, complex content no longer needs to be problematic for the supervisor who has a limited background in mathematics. To illustrate, the next section follows each skill from the elementary school classroom to the high school classroom.

Computation and Application Skills in Algebra

The development of algebra skills begins in the elementary school classroom (Carpenter, Franke, & Levi, 2003). For example, $2 + 2 = ?$, where students are required to fill in the blank with the correct answer, is a common type of computation problem in early elementary classrooms. However, many elementary teachers use a variation of the same problem that looks like this: $2 + ? = 4$. Thus, a simple arithmetic problem becomes an algebra problem. In secondary math classrooms, this same problem could look like this: $2 + x = 4$. To solve, middle school students subtract two from both sides:

$2(-2) + x = 4(-2)$

$0 + x = 2$

$x = 2$

Obviously, algebra problems do become somewhat more complex. By incorporating additional operations such as multiplication, secondary students have the opportunity to take the next step by learning to solve a two-step algebra problem. A two-step problem looks like this: $2x-4 = 12$. In this problem, the student needs to be able to see two operations, multiplication ($2x$) and subtraction ($2x-4$), and then be able to determine in which order each operation should be carried out. The order of operations then leads into the order of the steps necessary for the student to solve.

$2x-4 = 12$.

Step 1: $2x-4 + 4 = 12 + 4$

Step 2: $2x + 0 = 16$

Step 3: $2x = 16$

Step 4: $2x/2 = 16/2$

Step 5: $x = 8$.

The final step in developing algebra concepts is applying these skills to solve a real-world problem. Mathematics textbooks call these *story* problems. For example, a person preparing a recipe that requires 18 ounces of tomato paste finds that tomato paste is only sold in 4-ounce cans. How many cans need to be purchased for the recipe? Solving this problem requires several skills: problem solving, reading comprehension, and computation. For each can purchased, the buyer receives 4 ounces of tomato paste; mathematically, 4 × (the number of cans purchased). Since we need a total of 18 ounces, 4 × (the number of cans purchased) = 18. Using the algebraic convention of using x to represent what we do not know, our mathematical statement becomes $4x = 18$. The student is now ready to find a solution to the problem.

It should be noted that this problem, to more accurately represent a real-world problem, has a catch. The *algebraic* solution to the problem is 4½. But, because stores do not sell ½ cans of tomato paste, the *actual* answer requires the cook to purchase 5 cans of tomato five paste because four cans would not be enough.

Geometry

The development of geometry skills follows a path similar to the development of algebra skills. A common activity in early childhood classrooms requires students to recognize patterns. Common manipulatives for facilitating this type of activity are cards and blocks. The teacher places blocks in a particular order according to a criterion such as color or shape, and students are asked to use a separate set of blocks to duplicate that pattern. By the early elementary grades (1–2), students are matching names such as *square* and *triangle* to the shapes they have been studying.

As geometry transitions to the secondary arena, students begin exploring not just the shapes and their names, but also their attributes. For example, to learn the difference between a square and a rectangle, students must understand the properties of each shape. Then students will understand that the sides of a square all have equal length; the sides of a rectangle do not. This discovery leads to the geometric concept of congruent objects. Congruence simply means that two figures have the same exact size and shape.

In high school geometry classes, students generally extend their knowledge of shapes in two ways. First, in addition to congruence of figures, students begin exploring figures that are similar. Figures are similar if they are exactly the same shape, but not necessarily the same size. Second, high school students are introduced to writing proofs. A proof is a series of statements that uses either deductive reasoning or inductive reasoning to demonstrate that a given statement is true. Some high school students find proof writing especially challenging because writing a proof requires both knowledge of mathematical concepts and reasoning ability. The development of reasoning ability, a key component of problem solving, should be a part of the mathematics curriculum from the beginning of elementary school.

Application:
Another Word for Problem Solving

Perhaps the most important thread in the PreK–12 mathematics curriculum, and an area addressed at every level of the NCTM standards, is the development of problem solving skills. The National Council of Teachers of Mathematics (2000b) defines problem solving as "engaging in a task for which the solution *method* is not known in advance" (emphasis added) and asserts that "problem solving is an integral part of all mathematics learning, and so it should not be an isolated part of the mathematics program (p. 52).

From the use of simple manipulatives such as blocks or lollipops in elementary school, to graphing calculators in high school, students need to learn how to discover what strategies will help them to solve a mathematical problem. More importantly than memorizing rote strategies, students must learn the sometimes confusing language of mathematics. For example, do the phrases "take away" and "how many more" mean the same thing? Some students tend to associate the word "more" with addition. Unfortunately, "how many more" can be a signal that the student needs to subtract (Barnett-Clarke & Ramirez, 2003). This skill provides an important foundation for students learning to solve one of the most familiar of mathematical exercises, the story problem.

How does one determine what problem solving should look like at different levels? Application should be readily seen in all mathematics instruction, from the early grades through high school. Whether it is recognizing patterns in manipulatives in early childhood or story problems being solved in high school, the supervisor needs to focus on *process,* as opposed to attempting to understand content. Some questions the supervisor could engage the teacher in answering include the following:

- Are the manipulatives used appropriatly for the grade level?
- Is the mathematics teacher modeling the skills necessary to solve a story problem?
- Are the skills appropriate for the course?

A quick review of human development theory can help answer these questions.

Computation, application, and other mathematical skills can be enhanced through problem posing and solving. Teachers can be assisted in their delivery of the mathematics curriculum if they have a strong grasp of problem solving. Supervisors can be the mirror to practice by providing feedback to teachers' efforts at incorporating problem solving in the classroom.

The Supervisor's Scorecard

When teachers use problem solving as an instructional approach, they should do the following:

♦ Illustrate the relevance of finding solutions to problems.

♦ Identify the parts and processes of the formula and stages within the formula needed to solve the problem.

♦ Develop a systematic approach to solving the problem (some call this *small-step instruction*), ask questions, and engage students in calculating, graphing, or plotting step by step.

♦ Encourage students to apply different formulas for solving the problem—make connections to prior knowledge and skills.

♦ Make connections to real-life situations such as calculating the tax on a purchase or a certain discount percentage.

♦ Ask students to explain how a formula operates while they are applying the steps to the formula to a specific application.

♦ Write the steps to a problem on the blackboard while explaining formulas so that students can see and hear the explanation.

♦ Show alternate ways of solving the same problem.

♦ Provide opportunities for students to apply formulas to master skills.

♦ Monitor for understanding.

♦ Model the problem-solving process and possible strategies for solving problems.

♦ Form small cooperative groups to solve problems, monitor group work, and provide additional practice problems for groups that complete ahead of other groups.

♦ Increase the complexity of problems to be solved, and give opportunities for guided and independent practice.

♦ Follow up to homework with additional instruction.

Mathematics and Human Development Theory— Implications for Instruction

Success in mathematics learning is dependent, in part, on the student's ability to think abstractly. The level at which a student is able to think abstractly tends to limit her or his ability to symbolically represent quantities of objects (Kato, Kamii, Ozaki, & Nagahiro (2002). The development of abstract thinking is reflected in Piaget's Theory of Cognitive Development. The reader is encouraged to review the discussion of the cognitive and emotional development of students across the PreK–12 continuum offered in Chapter 6 and discussion of instructional strategies in Chapter 4.

Throughout the early elementary years (Piaget's preoperational stage; grades PreK–1), students are learning to think logically in one direction but are not usually capable of reversing the operation. Students in Piaget's preoperational stage work to make the transition from grouping and counting objects (placing 2 blocks next to 3 blocks and counting to 5) to solving the same problems using symbols ($2 + 3 = 5$). Older elementary students (grades 2–5) begin developing two important new skills: reversibility and conservation. Reversibility allows students to view subtraction as the inverse operation of addition. Conversion, the ability to perceive that a change in shape does not necessarily mean a change in quantity, permits students to view multiplication as repeated addition (e.g., $4 \times 2 = 2 + 2 + 2 + 2$).

As students start the middle school, many changes are occurring. Cognitively, these students are beginning to think abstractly. These young adolescents are entering Piaget's formal operational stage in which they are able to solve abstract problems logically and to become more scientific in their thinking (Woolfolk, 1998). Mathematics instruction in the secondary grades should provide students with multiple opportunities to develop and improve abstract thinking.

The NCTM recommends a rigorous curriculum of algebra and geometry to provide these opportunities. In the classroom, students in the middle grades should be learning two important skills. First, middle school students need to learn to build equations to represent real-life problems. In addition to numbers, these equations use letters to represent the unknown quantity for which the student must solve. The second skill requires students to transition from rote memorization of algorithms (established process carrying out an operation) to discovery of general strategies for problem solving.

The middle school years are important in keeping students interested in mathematical learning. The use of hands-on activities, combined with technology, can help keep students' interest in mathematics into high school. Mathematics instruction in high school should continue to offer students opportunities to improve their abstract thinking and problem-solving skills through the introduction of more advanced topics in the areas of algebra, geometry, trigonometry, and calculus.

Instructional Strategies
for Mathematics Learning

Reys, Lindquist, Lambdin, Smith, and Suydan (2004) report that "effective teachers use models, manipulatives, and technology when appropriate to explore problems and provide experiences that help children make sense of mathematics and help build their mathematical thinking" (p. 49). Research in mathematics education supports this assertion. Sowell (1989) concluded that mathematics lessons that include manipulatives are more likely to produce mathematical achievement in students. However, it is not enough to simply insert manipulatives into lesson plans. Scaffolding skills required for successfully completing the lesson are important for the use of manipulatives to be successful (Ross & Kurtz, 1993). For example, students must know the appropriate keystrokes before using the calculator to solve a problem.

Perhaps one of the most researched questions in mathematics instruction concerns the use of calculators. The NCTM Standards (2000b) support the use of technology at all levels of mathematics instruction. Ellington (2003) conducted a meta-analysis of the research in calculator use in mathematics classes. Results indicated that the research supports the assertion that students' operational skills and problem-solving skills improve with the use of calculators. Findings from research that examined the skill development of students who did not use calculators were mixed. Calculator use was also found to improve students' attitudes toward mathematics learning. Moreover, advanced placement calculus examinations include required calculator skills.

Computers also have myriad applications in the mathematics classroom. The software applications are too numerous to list. Computers are used in two important ways in mathematics classes: to reinforce concepts already learned and to extend learning through inquiry and exploration.

The Supervisor in the Mathematics Classroom

From manipulatives in elementary school to graphing calculators and computer software in high school, the mathematics classroom can be a challenging place for supervisors. Unfamiliar content can be problematic for even experienced administrators in conducting classroom observations. A review of the NCTM Standards (2000b) can provides some guidance for the principal without a mathematics background in supervising mathematics teachers. These standards suggest that quality mathematics instruction involves students as *active participants* in the processes of *computing, problem solving,* and *communicating.* The following sections offer some strategies that can help principals identify these behaviors in mathematics classrooms.

Computing

When considering the mathematics classroom, one of the first skills that comes to mind is computing. Are students able to add, subtract, multiply, and divide? For the principal observing in a mathematics classroom, the more relevant question is, what behaviors indicate that students are learning computing skills? Because of the nature of mathematics, computing is most often identified with the elementary grades. To document evidence of students learning computing skills, principals should look to see if students demonstrate the ability to

- compute using pencil and paper;
- represent and carry out computation using manipulatives;
- use technology such as calculators for more advanced computations.

The following teacher behaviors provide evidence that students are learning computational skills:

- Does the teacher provide opportunities for students to use a variety of tools to model computational skills?
- Does the teacher model techniques for checking the results of computations?
- Does the teacher demonstrate relationships between operations? (e.g., addition and subtraction are inverse operations.)

Further, principals need to look for evidence of teacher behaviors such as positive reinforcement and guidance that suggests that students are learning. Does the teacher monitor the students while they are working? Does the teacher help students who are struggling to find ways to catch up?

Problem Solving

For the mathematics teacher, student learning is not fully demonstrated by correct answers alone. Correct answers need to be accompanied by the process used to reach those answers. In other words, have the students learned how to identify the appropriate strategies for solving a given problem? The importance of problem solving in mathematics is twofold: for the student to demonstrate critical thinking skills and for the teacher to have the necessary information to be able to diagnose student difficulties. For the principal supervising a mathematics teacher, the following behaviors can help provide evidence that students are learning to problem-solve:

- Does the teacher talk about and model necessary steps for solving problems? For example, identify what the problem asks you to find;

decide on a strategy to use; determine whether or not the strategy was mathematically sound.

♦ Does the teacher identify cues that can help students determine the appropriate strategies for solving a given problem? For example, a teacher might ask, "What do you need to do when the problem says 'less than'?"

♦ Does the teacher model multiple ways of solving the same problem? For example, find out how many eggs are in two dozen by counting, by adding 12 and 12 together, or by multiplying 12 by 2.

♦ Are students *active* participants in the discussion of problem solving strategies? For example, "Teacher, could I have solved this problem using this technique instead of the first one we used?"

♦ Are students are given multiple opportunities to *actively* demonstrate the problem solving skills they have learned? For example, are students given opportunities to use chalkboard, overhead projector, or PowerPoint to share their solution to a problem with their classmates?

Although computing and problem-solving skills are central to mathematics classrooms, communicating mathematically helps provide the glue that holds mathematics instruction together.

Communicating

Learning computing and problem-solving skills require that students learn the language of mathematics, and learn how to use that language to communicate properly and accurately mathematical problems and solutions to others. Ask the following questions to help determine whether behaviors are present that provide evidence that students are learning to communicate mathematically:

♦ Does the teacher present and define relevant terminology as a part of mathematical lessons?

♦ Does the teacher use relevant terminology as a part of mathematical lessons?

♦ Do the students use the same terminology as *active* communicators of mathematics during the lesson?

To assist the principal observing in either an algebra or a geometry class, the information in Figure 7.2 can be helpful in keeping an eye focused on learning that would be appropriate at the high school level. Dr. James V. Foran, Director of Secondary School Development, and the High School Improvement Program Technical Assistance Group at the Maryland State Department of Education

(Gretchen Schultz, English; Linda Kaniecki, mathematics; Linda Yienger, social studies, and George Newberry, science) developed a series of "Look Fors" that can be modified to fit the needs of the context of the lesson being observed.

Figure 7.2. Administrator "Look Fors" in Algebra and Geometry

Rather than random lesson planning in algebra or geometry or simply following the table of contents of a textbook...

Teachers plan with the Core Learning Goals, Expectations, Indicators, and Assessment Limits in mind. Assessment Limits are extremely important because they prescribe the nonnegotiable topics of each concept that must be covered to ensure that students have been taught the material that will be tested. Teachers are invited to go as far beyond the Assessment Limits as time, their level of expertise, and the ability levels of the students they are teaching will allow.

Rather than simply doing problems in isolation...

Teachers involve students in real-world applications of mathematical concepts.

Rather than having students sit and listen...

Teachers actively engage students in mathematics through reading, writing, and oral communication.

Rather than students simply finding answers on their own...

Teachers foster more communication of mathematics by encouraging students to explain mathematical concepts to each other.

Rather than using technology for simple calculations...

Teachers encourage students to use technology for exploration and insight.

Rather than simply telling and explaining...

Teachers ask more questions to draw out high-level thinking, such as *why? explain? justify? elaborate?*

Rather than simply emphasizing correct answers...

Teachers engage students in mathematical concepts through investigations and discovery learning.

Rather than simply emphasizing rote multi-step manipulations...

Teachers relate skills and symbol manipulations to functions, tables, and graphs.

Rather than simply memorizing procedures...

Students frequently ask themselves appropriate questions and reasons to solve problems appropriate to the content of the course.

Rather than simply talking about mathematics in isolation...

Teachers help students make connections with previous knowledge in mathematics, as well as between mathematics and other disciplines.

Source: Dr. James V. Foran et al. (2000). Maryland State Department of Education. Retrieved November 25, 2003 from http://www.msde.state.md.us/hsimprovement/administratorlookfors.html Used with permission.

Two general strategies can be helpful for principals supervising in the mathematics classroom without the benefit of a mathematics background. First, focus on teacher and student behaviors that are consistent with the research on quality teaching instead of on the content of the lesson. Second, identify content expertise among the faculty and provide the resources necessary to empower those experts to become additional instructional leaders in the building.

Suggested Readings

Barnett-Clark, C., & Ramirez, A. (Eds.). (2003). *Number sense and operations in the primary grades: Hard to teach and hard to learn?* Portsmouth, NH: Heinemann.

Carpenter, T. P., Franke, M. L., & Levi, L. (2003). *Thinking mathematically: Integrating arithmetic & algebra in elementary school.* Portsmouth, NH: Heinemann.

Ellington, A. J. (2003). A meta-analysis of the effects of calculators on students' achievement and attitude levels in precollege mathematics classes. *Journal for Research in Mathematics Education, 34*(5), 433–463.

Kato, Y., Kamii, C., Ozaki, K., & Nagahiro, M. (2002). Young children's representations of groups of objects: The relationship between abstraction and representation. *Journal for Research in Mathematics Education, 33*(1), 30–45.

Reys, R. E., Lindquist, M. M., Lambdin, D. V., Smith, N. L., & Suydam, M. N. (2004). *Helping children learn mathematics.* (7th ed.). Hoboken, NJ: Wiley.

8

Supervision in the English/Language Arts Classroom

In this Chapter...

♦ Standards for English/language arts instruction
♦ English/language arts content across the PreK–12 continuum
♦ The supervisor in the English/language arts classroom
♦ English/language arts and human development theory—implications for instruction
♦ Instructional strategies for English/language arts learning

Reading is fundamental. Few people would disagree that reading *is* fundamental to learning. For students to solve story problems in mathematics, discover the past in social studies, or investigate the natural world in science, sound reading skills are essential. Because a teacher's ability to assess student learning relies on the students' ability to communicate what they have learned, speaking and writing skills are also critical. According to the United States Department of Education (2002), although federal funding for reading programs has more than doubled since 1996, reading scores have shown little change.

The *No Child Left Behind* act, enacted by Congress in 2001, mandates that every child in grades 3 through 8 will be tested in reading. The stakes in these exams are high; for example, schools deemed to be failing are listed publicly as failing and can be forced to pay the costs for students to transfer to "better" schools. The purposes of this chapter are to identify the standards prescribed for language arts instruction, to discuss appropriate teaching strategies for language arts classes across the PreK–12 continuum, and to offer suggestions for the principal who supervises language arts instruction.

Standards for English/Language Arts Instruction

The International Reading Association (IRA) and the National Council of Teachers of English (NCTE) have developed standards reprinted with permission by the International Reading Association and the National Council of Teachers of English (1996) in Figure 8.1.

Figure 8.1. IRA/NCTE Standards for English/Language Arts

1. Students read a wide range of print and non-print texts to build an understanding of texts, of themselves, and of the cultures of the United States and the world; to acquire new information; to respond to the needs and demands of society and the workplace; and for personal fulfillment. Among these texts are fiction and nonfiction, classic and contemporary works.

2. Students read a wide range of literature from many periods in many genres to build an understanding of the many dimensions (e.g., philosophical, ethical, aesthetic) of human experience.

3. Students apply a wide range of strategies to comprehend, interpret, evaluate, and appreciate texts. They draw on their prior experience, their interactions with other readers and writers, their knowledge of word meaning and of other texts, their word identification strategies, and their understanding of textual features (e.g., sound-letter correspondence, sentence structure, context, graphics).

4. Students adjust their use of spoken, written, and visual language (e.g., conventions, style, vocabulary) to communicate effectively with a variety of audiences and for different purposes.

5. Students employ a wide range of strategies as they write and use different writing process elements appropriately to communicate with different audiences for a variety of purposes.

6. Students apply knowledge of language structure, language conventions (e.g., spelling and punctuation), media techniques, figurative language, and genre to create, critique, and discuss print and non-print texts.

7. Students conduct research on issues and interests by generating ideas and questions, and by posing problems. They gather, evaluate, and synthesize data from a variety of sources (e.g., print and non-print texts, artifacts, people) to communicate their discoveries in ways that suit their purpose and audience.

8. Students use a variety of technological and information resources (e.g., libraries, databases, computer networks, video) to gather and synthesize information and to create and communicate knowledge.

9. Students develop an understanding of and respect for diversity in language use, patterns, and dialects across cultures, ethnic groups, geographic regions, and social roles.

10. Students whose first language is not English make use of their first language to develop competency in the English/language arts and to develop understanding of content across the curriculum.

11. Students participate as knowledgeable, reflective, creative, and critical members of a variety of literacy communities.

12. Students use spoken, written, and visual language to accomplish their own purposes (e.g., for learning, enjoyment, persuasion, and the exchange of information).

Jointly, the National Council of Teachers of English and the International Reading Association in the publication, *Standards for the English Language Arts* (1996), presented standards for English language instruction and reading across the PreK–12 continuum. These standards attempt to situate the student at the nexus of three dimensions of English language instruction: content, purpose, and development. Content, according to the *Standards for the English Language Arts* (1996), needs to address "what students should know and be able to do with the English language arts... [including] knowledge of written, spoken, and visual texts and of the processes involved in creating, interpreting, and critiquing such texts" (p. 13). The standards also cast the teacher as a learner: "By engaging with these standards, teachers will, we hope, also think and talk energetically about the assumptions that underlie their own classroom practices and those of their colleagues" (*Standards for the English Language Arts*, 1996, p. 24).

The IRA/NCTE provides a framework for understanding the organization and content of the standards. Standards 1 through 3 address reading; standards 4 through 6 transition to written and spoken language; standards 7 and 8 are referred to as "inquiry" standards (*Standards for the English Language Arts*, 1996, p. 26); standards 9 and 10 concern language in a diverse society, and standards 11 and 12 address students' individual experiences with language in terms of "their own purposes... learning, enjoyment, persuasion, and the exchange of information" (p. 3). The following discussion provides more in-depth information about these standards.

The Reading Standards (1–3)

The first three IRA/NCTE standards address reading skills. However, these standards do not prescribe pedagogy; rather they provide guidelines for selections of texts and for helping students understand and use a variety of approaches to reading. The IRA and the NCTE recommend that students read from "a variety of genres, including poetry, short stories, novels, plays, essays, biographies, and autobiographies" (*Standards for the English Language Arts*, 1996, p. 29). Moreover, the standards argue that students "need opportunities to explore and study many different kinds of printed texts, including contemporary and traditional novels, newspaper and magazine articles... historical documents [and] reference materials" (pp. 227–28).

Texts selected for study should also be reflective of today's diverse society to help students understand and appreciate cultures different from their own:

> The works students read should also reflect the diversity of the United States' population in terms of gender, age, social class, religion, and ethnicity. Students' understanding of our society and its history—and their ability to recognize and appreciate difference and diversity—are expanded when they read primary texts from across a wide demographic spectrum. (*Standards for the English Language Arts*, 1996, p. 28)

The *Standards for the English Language Arts* (1996) also asserts that teaching students varied reading strategies to ensure comprehension of a variety of texts is "of the greatest importance" (p. 32). By learning to interpret and formulate responses to those texts, students explore their own feelings and values (p. 33).

Standards for Written and Spoken Language Arts

In standards 4 through 6 the NCTE and IRA argue for language arts instruction that builds students' awareness of the need for multiple language forms and the development of the discretion to know when each should be used. These language forms should include both formal and informal forms:

> To ensure that they [students] can communicate effectively with a wide range of audiences, all students need to learn... standard English.... [A]ll students need to have standard English in their repertoire of language forms, and to know when they should use it. When students engage in discussions of when and where [standard English] should be used, they further their knowledge of audience, purpose, and context. (*Standards for the English Language Arts*, 1996, p. 34)

This need for standard English is addressed in terms of written as well as spoken English. Language arts teachers are urged to help students discover the components and process of writing. Students need to "recognize how to adapt tone, style, and content for the particular task at hand" (*Standards for the English Language Arts,* 1996, p. 35) and that "in reality, the writing process is recursive, not linear" (p. 36).

The sixth standard introduces the need for knowledge of the conventions of language, including punctuation and spelling. Further, the idea of *viewed* texts is introduced: "Students who work with films, for example, become aware of editing strategies that are used to weave together individual scenes to produce a continuous narrative" (*Standards for the English Language Arts,* 1996, p. 37). Comprehension is cast as only one component of written, spoken, and viewed texts. Students also need to develop the ability to critique and revise texts as well.

The Inquiry Standards

The inquiry standards urge language arts teachers to help students learn the skills necessary to apply a variety of communication skills to real-world needs to find information and solve problems: "It is essential that students acquire a wide range of abilities and tools for raising questions, investigating concerns, and solving problems" (*Standards for the English Language Arts,* 1996, p. 38). Although standard 7 addresses the mechanics of research (identifying a problem, collecting and analyzing data, and communicating the results), standard 8 speaks to the students' need to locate information using a variety of sources and technologies.

The Diversity Standards

Perhaps one of the issues most often discussed in education today is the need to honor the ever-increasing diversity found in America's classrooms. Standard 9 mandates that language arts teachers provide instruction that gives students the opportunity to explore cultures different from their own. Language is portrayed as a key in this endeavor:

> Language is a powerful medium through which we develop social and cultural understanding, and the need to foster this understanding is growing increasingly urgent as our culture becomes more diverse. Students deserve and need learning environments that respect cultural, racial, and ethnic differences. (*Standards for the English Language Arts,* 1996, p. 41)

Standard 10 addresses the learning of students for whom English is not their first language. This standard urges language arts teachers to provide instruction that helps students to succeed not only in language arts classes but across the entire curriculum.

Standards Addressing Students' Individual Experiences

The final two IRA/NCTE standards address language arts in terms of the students' individual experiences. Standard 11 describes the need for students to "participate as knowledgeable, reflective, creative, and critical members of a variety of literary communities" (*Standards for the English Language Arts*, 1996, p. 44). A literary community is defined as a group who share a common interest in a particular area of media. The term *area* can refer to a genre (e.g., novels, western films) or a writer or artist (e.g., John Knowles, Alfred Hitchcock).

The final standard promotes instruction that helps instill in students the desire to "use spoken, written, and visual language to accomplish their own purposes" (*Standards for the English Language Arts,* 1996, p. 45). This desire is cultivated by language arts teachers for the long term: "This final standard is clearly related to the ideal of producing lifelong learners—a goal that goes beyond the school years" (*Standards for the English Language Arts,* 1996, p. 45)

English/Language Arts Curriculum Across the PreK–12 Continuum

To discuss language arts curriculum in PreK–12 schools would require some agreement concerning just what the phrase "language arts" should include. According to the *Standards for the English Language Arts* (1996), the language arts include "reading, writing, listening, speaking, viewing, and visually representing" (p. 1). An examination of the *Standards for the English Language Arts* reveals two themes for language arts curriculum: students should be introduced to a variety of language conventions and texts chosen for use in class should be representative of our diverse society.

The very thought of English/language arts instruction tends to conjure thoughts of grammar worksheets to be completed, essays to be written, and literature to be read. In other words, standard English is the rule of the day. However, *Standards for the English Language Arts* (1996) advocates for instruction that introduces students to additional language conventions, "the informal... talk used among close friends gathered on the playground to discuss a basketball game is different from the more fully developed talk used with a teacher when discussing a piece of writing (pp. 33–34).

Although curriculum content is usually mandated by state law, language arts teachers need to select materials that reflect the growing diversity of American society. However, care must be taken in selecting texts from diverse cultures. Cox (1999) argues that

> when teaching with literature, teachers should choose works written
> by members of diverse groups who write about the struggle for iden-

tity in a white-dominated society... [and that the] group itself would choose and that show it as dynamic and active. (p. 77)

The *Standards for the English Language Arts* (1996) asserts two reasons why diversity in materials is essential in the language arts curriculum. First, using culturally diverse texts creates opportunities to teach students respect for different cultures. Second, the study of culturally diverse texts provides a foundation for interdisciplinary study.

Human Development Theory and Implications for English/Language Arts Instruction

Human development theory should inform both curriculum and instruction. Spodek and Saracho (1994) argue that knowledge of human development theory "can help us understand what... children are capable of knowing, how children come to know what they know at a particular age, and how they validate their knowledge" (p. 111). For language arts teachers, it is important to realize how quickly spoken language skills are developed. Charlesworth (2004) asserts, "The average child has achieved nearly adult language facility by the age of four" (p. 366).

The development of spoken language helps prepare a foundation for children to learn to read. Moreover, research suggests that story knowledge is also important to the development of reading skills. Children with story skills understand that a story has a beginning, a middle, and an end, and that a story has characters, a plot, a setting, and themes (McGee, Charlesworth, Check, & Check (1982). Reading instruction in the elementary grades also provides significant motivation for teachers to build partnerships with parents. Reading skills can be enhanced through such partnerships. Research suggests that children who are read to tend to learn to read earlier (Clark, 1984; Durkin, 1966). The implications this statement has for a classroom full of learners, especially in light of heightened accountability under *No Child Left Behind,* are daunting. Children's success on any standardized test depends heavily on their ability to read.

Although language development in the elementary grades is important, language skills can and should continue to develop during the middle and high school years. As students enter adolescence, they develop the ability to understand abstract words such as *finance.* Further, secondary students are able to distinguish subtle differences in tone and motivation in communication. For example, unlike their elementary counterparts, most adolescents can differentiate between good-natured kidding and taunting (Gardner, 1982).

Instructional Strategies
for English/Language Arts Classroom Learning

As with other disciplines, instruction in the language arts classroom benefits from a variety of instructional methods. These include small and large group instruction, direction instruction, cooperative learning, and inquiry (Cox, 1999).

The Supervisor's Scorecard

While visiting a teacher using the cooperative learning strategy, the supervisor can track data across several areas:

♦ *Specifying objectives for the lesson:* Both an academic objective and a social skills objective should be specified.

♦ *Making preinstructional decisions:* These decisions include size of groups, how students will be assigned to groups, what materials will be needed, and how the room will be arranged.

♦ *Explaining the task and positive interdependence:* The assignment is clearly defined including explanation of required concepts to be used, criteria for success, and individual accountability. Positive interdependence is emphasized.

♦ *Monitoring students' learning and intervening within the groups:* Through monitoring the group activities, the teacher will be able to determine individual student involvement. When necessary, the teacher intervenes to facilitate completion of task and interaction patterns of the group.

♦ *Evaluating students' learning and helping students process how well their group functioned:* Both student learning and group interaction are evaluated by the teacher, followed by student evaluation (Johnson & Johnson, 1994).

The following section describes instructional methods identified by research as effective for language arts instruction at the elementary and secondary levels and provides snapshots illustrating their applications in the classroom.

Language Arts in the Elementary Grades

Spodek and Saracho (1994) identify four goals of language arts instruction in the elementary grades:

1. *Verbal communication skills* to communicate their wants needs, ideas, and feelings as well as to receive similar communications from other people

2. *A rich language repertoire* by learning about the variety of styles and usage of language that are available to them

3. *An ability to use language to influence and be influenced*—the appropriate use of language, especially as a substitute for physical movements, is one of the most important social skills young children can learn

4. *Personal satisfaction in and an aesthetic appreciation of language*—children need to learn to use literature, poetry, creative dramatics, and other forms of expression to derive personal satisfaction. (pp. 298–299)

To reach these goals for language arts instruction, a variety of teaching strategies can be considered, and Combs (1996) promotes the need for elementary language arts teachers to use various teaching strategies in supporting children's reading and writing skills. Among the skills discussed by Combs are reading aloud to children, independent recreational reading, writer's workshops, and large- and small-group literature study.

Reading Aloud

Reading aloud provides students with the opportunity to develop and practice a variety of communications skills by interacting with the teacher, other students, and a story. Using nondirected questions, the language arts teacher facilitates group discussion; directed questions permit the teacher to monitor individual students' skills. Cox (1999) provides four guidelines for reading aloud:

1. Use reading aloud several times a day. In addition to modeling reading for children, reading aloud can help settle students and create a calm atmosphere in the classroom.

2. Reading dramatically demonstrates a love for reading and books. For variety, invite others, such as counselors, administrators, or students, to be readers.

3. Using predictable pattern books, such as Dr. Seuss, helps promote participation.

4. Reading "big books" is a good idea. This helps students feel comfortable in the classroom and allows students to see and follow the text. (pp. 135–136)

Research has identified several ways in which reading aloud helps children develop literacy skills. When read to, children learn how the activity of reading occurs (Smith, 1978). Clay (1979) argues that reading aloud to children helps them to understand that books have a beginning, a middle, and an end, and to understand that concept of authorship.

Independent Reading

The basis for using independent reading is found in the constructivist literature, which asserts that students need to be active participants, especially through hands-on activities, in their learning. Cox (1999) points out that independent reading "provides for individual differences in interest and ability and emphasizes construction of meaning while reading actual texts" (p. 299). However, Zarrillo (1989) warns that elementary language arts teachers may be reluctant to use independent reading because of inadequate administrative support, discomfort with the idea that each student is working at his own pace, inadequate training on implementation, and fear of standardized testing.

Writer's Workshops

A writer's workshop is an approach to teaching writing skills in which the teacher begins with a short, whole-class discussion of the day's lesson, followed by independent work time, and concluded with a review of the day's lesson and a preview of tomorrow's lesson. About 70% of the lesson time should used for the independent work time (Combs, 1996). By concentrating writing instruction on student work time, the workshop approach to writing instruction provides opportunities for teachers to monitor students' progress, offer individualized help, and use authentic assessment of student work.

Large- and Small-Group Literature Study

Another useful strategy for teaching language arts in the elementary classroom is the use of large- and small-group literature groups. Short and Pierce (1990) refer to these groups as literature circles and define them as groups of children who share an interest in a common book or theme. These groups can either be student-led or teacher-led (Heibert & Colt, 1989) and can provide concentrated instruction about literary elements, a specific author, an illustrator, or a genre (Combs, 1996). Learning in literature circles can be extended by having students keep response logs, conferencing with the students about their book, or by having students present their books to the entire class using drama or music (Cox, 1999).

Language Arts Instruction in the Secondary Classroom

Many of the skills taught in the secondary language arts classroom are similar to those taught in the elementary classroom. For this reason, many of the teaching strategies used in the elementary are also appropriate for secondary classrooms. Among these strategies are small group discussion of literature, journal writing, storytelling, and writing workshops. However, use of these strategies and the content selected in the secondary classroom should reflect the students' developmental levels.

Maxwell and Meiser (2001) suggest combining skills such as reading comprehension and writing through small group literature-based activities. For example, students could write a position paper describing what is right and wrong with Jonas's society in *The Giver*. Through this learning activity, the student is provided an opportunity to demonstrate reading comprehension skills and composition skills. This small group activity can lead into a large group discussion the content of The Giver or possibly a class review of writing skills.

The Supervisor in the English/Language Arts Classroom

At first blush, supervising in the English/language arts classroom might seem straightforward. After all, the principal knows the language and, with English study mandatory in both high school and college, at least some familiarity with course content could be assumed. In today's high accountability environment, however, the importance of examining supervisory behaviors specific to the English/language arts classroom should not be overlooked. The framework of the *Standards for the English Language Arts* (1996) suggests that principals need to examine teacher and student behaviors in the English/language arts classroom in terms of reading, writing, speaking, and viewing.

Reading (Literature)

Whether in elementary or secondary classrooms, principals make informed judgments about teaching and learning based on data that describe whether or not students are actively involved in the lesson. Perhaps more important, what teacher behaviors motivate students to participate? Here are some behaviors for which the principal might look:

◆ Does the teacher involve the students in the selection of texts?

◆ Does the teacher connect the texts to concepts familiar to the students (scaffolding)?

- Does the teacher use directed questions to involve all learners in discussions?
- Does the teacher give students the opportunity to help each other learn from the text?

Writing

Students can and should use writing skills across the curriculum. However, the primary venue for learning how to write is the English/language arts classroom. Examples of teacher behaviors principals should look for during writing instruction might include the following:

- Does the teacher actively model different writing skills?
- Does the teacher give each student feedback on his/her writing?
- Does the teacher give students the opportunity to critique each other's writing?
- Does the teacher connect writing assignments to literature being read in class?
- Does the teacher connect writing assignments to concepts familiar to students?
- Does the teacher involve students in selecting topics for writing assignments?

When supervising a language arts class during a writing lesson, the principal needs to be aware the writing is a recursive process, not a linear one. The writer goes back and forth between stages instead of progressing from one stage to another in lockstep (Maxwell & Meiser, 2001). Modeling and feedback should be evident at each stage in the writing process.

Speaking and Viewing

In addition to reading and writing, English/language arts teachers plan lessons that address students' abilities to use appropriate language conventions in spoken communications. Some teacher behaviors to look for might include the following:

- Does the teacher model appropriate use of language conventions in his/her spoken communications?
- Does the teacher provide opportunities for students to demonstrate the ability to use appropriate language conventions (e.g., class presentations)?

◆ Does the teacher involve the students in selecting topics for class-room presentations?

◆ Does the teacher encourage or require students to use technology in their presentations?

◆ Does the teacher encourage students to incorporate their cultures in their presentations?

While these lists certainly are not meant to be exhaustive, they do provide some important guidelines for principals when supervising in English/language arts classrooms.

Figure 8.2 provides additional guidelines developed by Dr. James V. Foran, Director of Secondary School Development, and the High School Improvement Program Technical Assistance Group at the Maryland State Department of Education (Gretchen Schultz, English; Linda Kaniecki, mathematics; Linda Yienger, social studies, and George Newberry, science).

Figure 8.2. Administrator "Look Fors" in English

Rather than random lesson planning in English or simply following the table of contents of a textbook…

Teachers plan with the Core Learning Goals, Expectations, Indicators, and Assessment Limits in mind. Assessment Limits are extremely important because they prescribe the nonnegotiable topics of each concept that must be covered to ensure that students have been taught the material that will be tested. Teachers are invited to go as far beyond the assessment limits as time, their level of expertise, and the ability levels of the students they are teaching will allow.

Rather than interpreting texts for students…

Teachers encourage students to construct their own meaning from texts, to ask their own questions, and to synthesize multiple peer interpretations.

Rather than accept any opinion about a text…

Teachers require students to defend their opinions with appropriate textual support.

Rather than assign students to read and answer questions about a text…

Teachers model, guide, and direct students in using appropriate strategies to prepare for reading, to ask their own questions, to probe and elaborate on meaning, to make personal connections to text, and to apply an understanding of texts to real world situations.

Rather than reading texts in isolation...

Teachers model and guide students in making connections among texts, noting their similarities and differences.

Rather than merely giving students an assignment to write on a given topic...

Teachers model, guide, and direct students in using all steps of a writing process: prewriting, drafting, and revising.

Rather than assigning all texts...

Teachers provide opportunities and guidance for students to select and study their own appropriate texts.

Rather than scoring student papers only with letter or percentage grades...

Teachers guide students in scoring constructed responses with rubrics–which are presented with the assignment.

Rather than being the sole audience for student writing...

Teachers also give students opportunities to write for authentic audiences, such as elementary or middle school students or newspapers.

Rather than being the sole evaluators of student writing...

Teachers give students opportunities to share their writing with their peers for review and evaluation and to develop their own criteria for evaluation.

Rather than criticize student writing...

Teachers offer revision suggestions early in the process, guide students in using peer response to suggest revisions, assist students in revision techniques for more effective development and communication of ideas, and engage students in the use of appropriate resources to correct and confirm their revisions.

Rather than assign discrete language exercises from traditional language handbooks...

Teachers instruct students to examine how words are used in light of their context, especially in works of literary merit and in their own writing.

Rather than teach lengthy units on grammatical structures and mechanics...

Teachers emphasize effectiveness over correctness and address the needs of the students through a variety of instructional strategies, such as a mini-lesson focused on one type of construction or usage.

Rather than evaluate texts *only* for their structures or literary elements…

Teachers also examine and discuss with students the effectiveness of the language choices made by the writers, including student writers.

Source: Dr. James V. Foran et al. (2000). Maryland State Department of Education. Retrieved November 25, 2003 from http://www.msde.state.md.us/hsimprovement/administratorlookfors.html. Used with permission.

The skills learned in the English/language arts classroom can and should provide basic skills essential for learning across the curriculum. Along with the new levels of federally mandated accountability, supervising in the English/language arts classroom should become a priority. English/language arts teachers need ongoing opportunities to learn how they can help students build connections between reading, writing, speaking, and viewing skills. Moreover, ongoing professional development can also assist English/language arts teachers to help students discover the connections between language arts and the other core disciplines.

Suggested Readings

Combs, M. (1996). *Developing competent readers and writers in the primary grades.* Englewood Cliffs, NJ: Merrill.

Cox, C. (1999). *Teaching language arts: A student- and response-centered approach* (3rd ed.). Boston: Allyn & Bacon.

Durkin, D. (1966). *Children who read early.* New York: Teachers College Press.

Maxwell, R. J., & Meiser, M. J. (2001). *Teaching English in the middle and secondary schools* (3rd ed.). Upper Saddle River, NJ: Merrill.

Zarrillo, J. (1989). Teacher's interpretations of literature-based reading. *Reading Teacher, 43*(1), 22–28.

9

Supervision in the Social Studies Classroom

In this Chapter...

♦ Standards for social studies instruction

♦ Social Studies content across the PreK–12 continuum

♦ Social Studies and human development theory—implications for instruction

♦ Instructional strategies for social studies learning

♦ The principal in the social studies classroom

America's public schools are now more diverse than ever. In the Los Angeles (California) County Schools, one-third of the student population is considered English language learners (learning English as a second language). These students represent more than 90 languages (Los Angeles County Schools, 2003). World events, combined with instant, worldwide communications, bring exotic places into America's living rooms every day. Being an informed citizen in today's world demands a wide knowledge of places, people, and customs. Social studies instruction can and should be planned as an important role in helping school children learn about and appreciate cultures different from their own.

Social studies, as defined in PreK–12 schools, encompasses a variety of disciplines including history, geography, government or civics, economics, psychology, and, in some cases, sociology and anthropology. The purposes of this chapter are to introduce the standards for social studies instruction, discuss instructional strategies appropriate to the social studies classroom, and provide strategies for the principal supervising in the social studies classroom.

Standards for Social Studies Instruction

The National Council for the Social Studies (NCSS) has provided a set of standards for social studies instruction in PreK–12 schools. These standards are divided into three major areas: subject matter standards, pedagogical standards, and programmatic standards for initial licensure. Because the programmatic standards address preservice preparation of social studies teachers only, this book focuses on the subject matter and pedagogical standards only. Figure 9.1 offers a summary of these standards.

Figure 9.1. NCSS Standards

Subject Matter Standards

Thematic Standards. Social studies teachers should possess the knowledge, skills, and dispositions to organize and provide instruction at the appropriate school level for the study of the following:

- Culture and Cultural Diversity
- Time, Continuity, and Change
- People, Places, and Environments
- Individual Development and Identity
- Individuals, Groups, and Institutions
- Power, Authority, and Governance
- Production, Distribution, and Consumption
- Science, Technology, and Society
- Global Connections
- Civic Ideals and Practices

Disciplinary Standards. Teachers licensed to teach any of the following disciplines at all school levels should possess the knowledge, capabilities, and dispositions to organize and provide instruction at the appropriate school level for the study of said discipline(s):

- History
- Geography
- Civics and Government
- Economics
- Psychology

Pedagogical Standards. Social studies teachers should possess the knowledge, capabilities, and dispositions to provide learning opportunities that demonstrate instruction competence in the following areas:

- Learning and Development
- Differences in Learning Styles
- Critical Thinking, Problem Solving, and Performance Skills
- Active Learning and Motivation
- Inquiry, Collaboration, and Supportive Classroom Interaction
- Planning Instruction
- Assessment
- Reflection and Professional Growth
- Professional Leadership

Source: Reprinted by permission of the National Council for the Social Studies. Available online: http://www.socialstudies.org/standards/teachers

Thematic Standards for Social Studies Teachers

The thematic standards of the National Council for the Social Studies (1997) offer expectations of the knowledge and skills needed for social studies instruction that support active student learning. The threads of critical thinking and active learning are woven throughout the thematic standards. Situated against the backdrop of diversity, the standards provide a framework for understanding the cultural, historical, social, political, economic, and scientific development of different peoples.

The first thematic standard provides a framework for understanding the remaining nine standards by situating these standards in the context of a multicultural society. Standards 2 and 3 provide the frameworks of chronology and setting. Social studies teachers are expected to help students learn how to view events and persons in the contexts of time and place. Moreover, students need to learn how knowledge of time and place affect the perception of persons and events. For example, student may not fully understand the importance of terraced farming in ancient Greece without a knowledge of the mountains on which many of the Greeks lived.

Standards 4 and 5 address the social development of humankind. Beginning with individual identity and continuing with group and institutional identities, these standards ask teachers to examine the cognitive, social, and emotional development of individuals and the roles that education and religions play in supporting that development. Standards 6 through 8 provide guidelines for the study of political, economic, technological, and scientific development and how each of these relates to the others. Standard 9 addresses the global view of society. Social studies teachers are asked to help students in discovering the interdependence and connectedness of world cultures. The final thematic standard (10) requires students to discover ways that they can apply learning from the first nine standards in local settings such as their school or community.

Disciplinary Standards

In addition to the interdisciplinary thematic standards, the NCSS also provides discipline specific standards for five areas: history, geography, civics and government, economics, and psychology. These standards continue the threads of critical thinking and active learning. Each disciplinary standard is defined in terms of learner expectations, teacher expectations, and school applications.

History Standards

The NCSS history standards address two major topics: the tools used by historians to study history and historical content. The first five history standards address the tools of the historian's trade. Standards one through three address how historians think: chronologically and analytically. Teachers are expected to assist students to learn to analyze narratives for content and to recognize cause and effect relationships. One instructional method suited for this type of learning is the Socratic Seminar (see Chapter 4 for elaboration on this instructional method). The following Socratic Seminar Observation Form and other materials (Figure 9.2), reproduced with permission from the Seventh-Day Adventist North American Division Office of Education, can assist supervisors to track information while observing during a Socratic Seminar.

Figure 9.2. Socratic Seminar Observation Form

Observer: _____ Date: _____

Reading item: _____

Opening question: _____

_____

_____

_____

Persons Observed	Uses Text	Listens +/0/–	Responds to Questions	Paraphrases	Asks Questions	Defers	Comments: Numbers or Words

Comments—Use these numbers for comments.

1. Needs to speak more.

2. Playful

3. Calls out, interrupts.

4. Plays with name card and other things.

5. Needs to listen more carefully—asks for repeated comments.

6. Has an excellent idea.

7. Asks good questions.

8. Outstanding participation—includes responding, asking questions, paraphrasing, and deferring.

What is the best idea you heard in the seminar?

_____

_____

_____

_____

How would you rate the seminar? (Check One)

____ Excellent (Everyone participated, listened, had good ideas, did not interrupt.)

____ Good (Generally, everyone participated but the seminar could have better ideas and behavior.)

____ Fair (Side talk, interruptions, students distracted.)

____ Poor (Lots of side talk, interruptions, and rude behavior.)

How many times did the facilitator have to stop the seminar? _____

Techniques used in conducting and applying historical research are introduced in the standards 4 and 5 to help students discover how examining the past can help inform them about the present and the possibilities of the future.

Standards 6 through 8 transition the social studies teachers' focus from the historian's craft to historical content. The United States and North America are addressed in standard 6, and Western and world civilization are addressed in standard 7. The final history standard, 8, expects teachers and students to examine history from a global perspective from social, political, economic, and cultural perspectives.

Geography Standards

The NCSS geography standards can be categorized into two major groups: physical geography and human geography. Standards 1 through 7 address the physical characteristics of the earth (e.g., ecosystems, mountains, and rivers), how these features were formed, and how they affect human life. The remaining 10 standards address geography from the human perspective. Teachers are expected to facilitate student discovery of human migration patterns, human modification of the physical world, and the processes of human settlement. Throughout the geography standards, teachers are urged to deliver instruction that encourages students to analyze and to interpret the ongoing relationship between humankind and the physical world.

Civics and Government Standards

The standards for the study of civics and government address three areas: a general overview of government, the United States system of government, and the rights and responsibilities of citizenship. The first standard encourages teachers and students to explore the origins of governmental power, the roles of government, and to examine different types of governments. Standards 2 through 4 examine United States government beginning with a broad overview, transitioning to an examination of the United States Constitution, and concluding with a look at the relationship of the United States to the rest of the world.

The final two standards for civics and government leave the broad view of government and focus on the individual. Standard 5 addresses the rights and responsibilities of citizens, while the final standard, 6, urges and exploration of opportunities to exercise the rights and responsibilities afforded in the United States. Social studies teachers are also encouraged to help students find opportunities for exercising their rights as citizens in their school and community.

Economics

Meeting the NCSS standards for economics requires instruction that addresses four major topics: goods and services (standards 1 through 5), market forces (standards 6 through 8), capital and investing (standards 9 through 13), and government influences on economics (standards 14 through 18). Instruction for goods and services would introduce students to topics such as limited resources, cost/benefit analysis, allocation, incentives, and trade.

The market forces standards address an overview of market forces, supply, demand, and the influence of institutions such as banks, corporations, unions, and nonprofit organizations on markets. Capital and investing studies include a basic introduction to investing, interest, inflation, and financing a business and entrepreneurship. The final section of the standards, government influences, introduces students to governmental agencies such as the Federal Reserve that influence the United States' economy, unemployment, and taxes.

Psychology

The final set of disciplinary standards provides expectations for psychology classes. These standards prescribe instruction that addresses topics that include human development theory, personality, mental health, and research techniques used by psychologists. Meeting standard 1 requires instruction through which teachers and students explore cognitive, emotional, and social development theories. Standards 2 through 6 address coping behaviors, memory, personal traits, and identity. Mental and emotional health are addressed in standard 7, and standards 8 through 11 address psychological research and its application to practice.

Social Studies Curriculum Across the PreK–12 Continuum

A discussion of the social studies curriculum would, of necessity, proposes the question, "What is social studies?" Formulating such a definition is the subject of an ongoing debate (Lybarger, 1991). Barr, Barth, and Shermis (1978) identified three traditions through which social studies can be defined: social studies as citizenship transmission, social studies as social science, and social studies as reflective inquiry. A comprehensive definition of social studies was offered by the House of Delegates of the NCSS:

> Social studies is the integrated study of the social sciences and humanities to promote civic competence. Within the school program, social studies provides coordinated systematic study drawing upon such disciplines as anthropology, economics, geography, history, law,

philosophy, political science, psychology,   religion, and sociology, as well as appropriate content from the humanities, mathematics, and natural sciences. The primary purpose of social studies is to help young people develop the ability to make informed and reasoned decision for the public good as citizens of a culturally diverse, democratic society in an interdependent world. (p. 194)

Based on this definition, it is apparent that today's social studies curriculum is complex. Because social studies is comprised of many disciplines, providing a general description of the curriculum taught in PreK–12 social studies class is problematic. However, the National Commission on Social Studies in Schools (1989) provided some guidance. This group asserted that social studies in 21st Century schools should assist students to develop

- ◆ civic responsibility and active civic participation;

- ◆ perspectives on their own life experiences so they see themselves as part of the larger human adventure in time and place;

- ◆ a critical understanding of the history, geography, economic, political, and social institutions, traditions, and values of the United States as expressed in both their unity and diversity;

- ◆ an understanding of other peoples and the unity and diversity of world history, geography, institutions, traditions, and values;

- ◆ critical attitudes and analytical perspectives appropriate to analysis of the human condition. (p. 6)

Three themes in the social studies curriculum for PreK–12 students are apparent: preparing students for the responsibilities of citizenship; fostering in children an appreciation and respect for cultures different from their own; and developing in children the ability to interpret political, economic, social, scientific, and technological events. When viewed against the backdrop of human development theory, the diversity within the social studies has implications for planning and delivering instruction.

Human Development Theory and Implications for Social Studies Instruction

Reviewing Piaget's theory of cognitive development and Erikson's theory of psychosocial development provides guidance for planning instruction in social studies classrooms. Piaget asserts that as children enter the early elementary grades they are still developing the ability to think logically. According to Erikson, these children explore their world through role playing. For the elementary school social studies teacher, students in the early elementary grades could benefit from being involved in simple simulations such as being a pilgrim or a Native American for Thanksgiving.

For children in the late elementary grades, diverse learning experiences will provide guidance as they work to determine their strengths. This is consistent with Erikson's belief that elementary school children need to find those things at which they can excel. Learning activities for these children need to provide them with opportunities to try a wide variety of skills. It is important for teachers at the upper elementary level to keep in mind that many of their students are still limited to concrete ideas. Sample activities could include holding a mock election or identifying ways students can be environmentally friendly at their school.

As students work their way through middle and high school, they develop the ability to think abstractly. Moreover, these young adolescents are busy trying to establish an identity. These students need learning activities that stretch their efforts to develop abstract thinking skills, provide opportunities to learn about themselves and their place in society, and to explore social issues relevant to them. Activities such as mock trials, panel discussions, and television/radio simulations are appropriate. To be able to deliver instruction this diverse, social studies teachers need to examine how these activities are planned and delivered.

Instructional Strategies for the Social Studies Classroom

Thorton (1991) refers to the social studies teacher as the "curricular-instructional gatekeeper" (p. 237) because the social studies teacher is expected to decide *how* to teach a varied collection of disciplines to a diverse collection of learners. Although social studies curriculum is diverse, research suggests that social studies teachers tend to depend on direct instruction and recitation for delivering instruction (Hertzberg, 1981).

However, the very nature of social studies suggests the need for varied teaching strategies in the classroom. These strategies should include cooperative learning, inquiry, and simulations (Kaltsounis, 1979; Savage & Armstrong, 1996).

Cooperative Learning in the Social Studies Classroom

According to the NCSS standards, one of the primary purposes of social studies instruction is to prepare students to be responsible citizens. Cooperative learning strategies can provide students with practical experience being a member of a group working together. In essence, properly conducted cooperative learning activities can provide students the opportunity to *practice* citizenship skills as they are learning *about* citizenship. Several types of cooperative learning activities are appropriate for social studies instruction: think-pair-share, inside-outside, and classroom debate.

In think-pair-share, students are first given a problem to think about individually. After a few minutes have elapsed, students exchange their thoughts in pairs. The final step provides each pair to share their ideas with the whole class (McTighe & Lyman, 1988). Think-pair-share can be used at any level. Examples of think-pair-share activities might include having elementary students brainstorm ways of improving the environment, asking middle school students to explore the limits of their first amendment rights, or having high school students explore causes of World War II.

Inside-outside method requires the social studies teacher to divide the class into two groups: the inside group and the outside group. The inside group is a traditional cooperative learning group. They have a question to address or a problem to solve, and each member of the group has a specific role in arriving at a solution. The outside group's job is to observe the workings of the inside group and take notes. When the inside group has completed its work, the two groups trade places. The inside group becomes the outside group, and vice versa. The activity culminates with a whole-class discussion in which solutions to the problem and observations of the problem-solving process are shared. With the inside-outside technique, students are not only learning content, they are also learning how to work as a part of a team (Savage & Armstrong, 1996), and they are developing creativity.

Inquiry in the Social Studies Classroom

Inquiry teaching requires students to take the lead in their own learning by conducting an investigation into a given problem or issue. Inquiry is particularly useful in teaching students to gather and analyze data (Kaltsounis, 1979). For example, an elementary social studies teacher could have students collect information about how lands and seas are depicted on maps and globes. From these data, the students could reach conclusions such as that the color blue is used to represent water (Savage & Armstrong, 1996). A middle school social studies teacher might have students collect data about world economies and life expectancies of different countries to investigate the connections between a nation's wealth and the health of its people. At the high school level, a psychology teacher could have students collect data about drug abuse among teens and form conclusions about the associated costs to society.

Simulations

In some ways a variation of cooperative learning, simulations can be a powerful way of giving students the opportunity to become an active participant in a historical or societal event. During a simulation, students "walk in another's shoes." Although complete reality is not possible, simulations help students to gain a more intimate view of the event being simulated. Savage and Armstrong (1996) identify four phases of simulations:

1. Overview—students are introduced to the simulation, the parts to be played, and what rules must be followed.

2. Training—students shown what they will be expected to do.

3. Activity—the simulation takes place.

4. Debriefing—assisted when needed by the teacher, students discuss what they learned. (p. 216)

Simulations can be effective learning activities at many levels. Students in the upper elementary grades could hold a mock city council meeting to better understand how their city operates. Middle school students might hold a mock presidential election, complete with a meeting of the Electoral College. A high school world history classroom could, for a day, be turned into a concentration camp for students studying the holocaust.

Two caveats should be offered for social studies teachers considering the use of simulations. First, the preparation for simulations can be time intensive. Materials and props must be obtained. Some simulations require a setting other than the classroom. In addition to securing the setting, arrangements to transport students to and from the classroom need to be made. Second, some activities such as a holocaust simulation can create strong emotion in the classroom. The teacher needs to consider the maturity of the students involved when deciding whether or not to use this type of activity in the classroom.

As stated earlier, one of the primary goals of social studies instruction is providing students with the opportunity to learn the skills of citizenship. By using active teaching methods such as cooperative learning, inquiry, and simulations, social studies teachers create an enriched environment in which students learn content and citizen skills simultaneously. For the principal, supervising teachers who use multiple teaching methods suggest multiple forms of data that can be collected during classroom observations. The following section provides some strategies for supervising in the social studies classroom.

The Supervisor in the Social Studies Classroom

The social studies classroom should provide the principal with opportunities to collect myriad types of observation data. Because a major goal for social studies instruction is to prepare students for active participation as citizens, principals should observe students *actively participating* in learning. Figure 9.3 provides additional guidelines developed by Dr. James V. Foran, Director of Secondary School Development, and the High School Improvement Program Technical Assistance Group at the Maryland State Department of Education (Gretchen Schultz, English; Linda Kaniecki, mathematics; Linda Yienger, social studies, and George Newberry, science).

Figure 9.3. Administrator "Look Fors" in American Government

Rather than random lesson planning in American government or simply following the table of contents of a textbook...

Teachers plan with the Core Learning Goals, Expectations, Indicators, and Assessment Limits in mind. Assessment Limits are extremely important because they prescribe the nonnegotiable topics of each concept that must be covered to ensure that students have been taught the material that will be tested. Teachers are invited to go as far beyond the Assessment Limits as time, their level of expertise, and the ability levels of the students they are teaching will allow.

Rather than a steady diet of "drill" and "kill" techniques...

Teachers utilize a variety of instructional strategies to reinforce the role of government in our lives.

Rather than an emphasis on simple recall of knowledge...

Teachers emphasize content application and higher level thinking skills in evaluating government.

Rather than giving assignments to reinforce facts...

Teachers frequently give writing assignments analyzing the functioning and effect of government.

Rather than assessing discrete knowledge...

Teachers assess understanding of concepts of government.

Rather than passively listening or reading texts on government...

Students are actively engaged in their own learning through hands-on activities in the classroom.

Rather than a steady diet of completing puzzles or worksheets as assessment items…

Students practice writing brief and extended constructed responses.

Rather than a steady diet of copying charts, lists, or organizers…

Students analyze charts, issues, and political cartoons.

Rather than simply taking low level quizzes…

Students demonstrate learning daily through classroom discussions and other informal assessment measures.

Rather than simply discussing government in the abstract…

Teachers help students make connections between government and the real world as well as with other disciplines.

Source: Dr. James V. Foran et al. (2000). Maryland State Department of Education. Retrieved November 25, 2003 from http://www.msde.state.md.us/hsimprovement/administratorlookfors.html. Used with permission.

Because principals supervise social studies teachers in diverse disciplines from elementary social studies to various high school classes including history, geography, psychology, economics, and sociology, some general tips for supervising in these classrooms can be helpful. The following tips are offered:

♦ Are the students actively involved in learning?

♦ Does the teacher give students opportunities to work together to learn?

♦ Do the learning activities have strong real-life applications or connections?

♦ Are students encouraged to express and to give support for their personal viewpoints?

♦ Does the teacher plan learning activities that require students to think critically rather than simply to recall facts?

Positive answers to these questions would indicate that students are actively engaged in learning and can help to prepare them to actively participate as citizens in their communities.

The social studies classroom should offer students many opportunities to practice skills they will need to become active citizens as adults. Active teaching strategies such as cooperative learning and simulations are time consuming to prepare and challenging to manage in the classroom. Teachers, especially those with limited experience using active teaching strategies in the classroom, need supervisory support for two reasons: to receive feedback that will help them improve in using these strategies and to ensure that students are on-task and learning.

Suggested Readings

Ellis, A. K. (1995). *Teaching and learning elementary social studies.* Boston: Allyn & Bacon.

Harris, D. (1997). Assessing discussion of public issues. In R. S. Evans & D. W. Saxe (Eds.), *Handbook on teaching social issues.* NCSS Bulletin 93. Washington, DC: National Council for Social Studies.

Marotrella, P. H. (1996). *Teaching social studies in middle and secondary schools.* Englewood Cliffs, NJ: Prentice Hall.

National Commission on Social Studies in Schools. (1989). *Charting a course: Social studies for the 21st Century.* Washington, DC: National Council for the Social Studies.

Savage, T. V., & Armstrong, D. G. (1996). *Effective teaching in elementary social studies* (3rd ed.). Englewood Cliffs, NJ: Merrill.

Stern, B. S. (2002). *Social studies: Standards, meaning & understanding.* Larchmont, NY: Eye On Education.

10

Supervision in the Science Classroom

In this Chapter...

- ◆ Standards for science instruction
- ◆ Science content across the PreK–12 continuum
- ◆ Science and human development theory—implications for instruction
- ◆ Instructional strategies for science learning
- ◆ The supervisor in the science classroom

Science is pervasive in society. Nationally, about 4.7 million scientists and technicians are employed in fields as diverse as agriculture, construction, financial services, manufacturing, transportation, and utilities (Division of Science Resources Statistics, 2002). Replenishing and even increasing this cadre of professionals begins with science education in PreK–12 schools and represents a daunting challenge to the nation's science teachers and those who supervise them.

Trends in student achievement in science suggest that there is much work to be done. The National Science Board provided the following statistics:

- ◆ Although 17-year-olds had higher science scores in 1999 that did their counterparts in 1982, the average 1999 score remained 10 points below the average score in 1969.

- ◆ Despite gains in scores of 9-year-olds and 13-year-olds since the early 1980s, average scores in 1999 are about the same as those in 1970.

- ◆ Boys outperformed girls in science achievement in 1999, but the difference was not significant.

- ◆ The science achievement gap between white students and their African-American and Hispanic counterparts narrowed between the years 1973 and 1999 but remains large. (National Science Board, 2002)

Meeting the challenges of science instruction in PreK–12 schools requires a partnership between science teachers and their principals. The purposes of this chapter are to discuss the *National Science Education Standards,* examine what these standards suggest for PreK–12 science curriculum, explore implications of human development theory to science instruction, suggest teaching strategies useful in the science classroom, and offer suggestions for principals supervising in science classrooms.

The National Science Education Standards

The standards endorsed by the National Science Teacher's Association for science instruction in PreK–12 schools are the *National Science Education Standards* (NSES), published in 1996 by the National Research Council (NRC). The National Research Council draws members from the National Academy of Science, The National Academy of Engineering, and the Institute of Medicine. These standards are divided into six subsections: Science Teaching Standards, Professional Development Standards, Assessment Standards, Science Content Standards, Science Education Program Standards, and Science Education System Standards. Figure 10.1 offers a summary of the NSES standards.

Figure 10.1. NSES Science Education Standards

National Science Education Standards

Science Teaching Standards. Teachers of science

- plan an inquiry-based science program for their students;

- guide and facilitate learning;

- engage in ongoing assessment of their teaching and of student learning;

- design and manage learning environments that provide students with time, space, and resources needed for learning science;

- develop communities of science learners that reflect the intellectual rigor of scientific inquiry and the attitudes of social values conducive to science learning;

- Actively participate in the ongoing planning and development of the school science program.

Standards for Professional Development for Teachers of Science. Professional development for teachers of science

♦ requires learning essential science content through the perspectives and methods of inquiry;

♦ requires integrating knowledge of science, learning, pedagogy, and students; also requires applying that knowledge to science teaching;

♦ requires building understanding and ability for lifelong learning;

♦ must be coherent and integrated.

Assessment Standards

♦ Assessments must be consistent with the decisions they are designed to inform.

♦ Achievement and opportunity to learn science must be assessed.

♦ The technical quality of the data collected is well matched to the decisions and actions taken on the basis of their interpretation.

♦ Assessments must be fair.

♦ The inferences made from assessments about student achievement and opportunity to learn science must be sound.

Science Content Standards

K–12: Science as Inquiry

As a result of activities in grades K–12, all students should develop

♦ abilities to do scientific inquiry;

♦ understanding about scientific inquiry.

K–4: Content Standards

Physical Science: All students should develop an understanding of

♦ properties of objects and materials;

♦ position and motion of objects;

♦ light, heat, electricity, and magnetism;

Life Science: All students should develop an understanding of

♦ the characteristics of organisms;

♦ life cycles of organisms;

♦ organisms and environments.

Earth and Space Science: All students should develop an understanding of

♦ properties of earth materials;

♦ objects in the sky;

- changes in the earth and sky.

Science and Technology: All students should develop

- abilities of technological design;
- understanding about science and technology;
- abilities to distinguish between natural objects and objects made by humans.

Science in Personal and Social Perspectives: All students should develop an understanding of

- personal health;
- characteristics of changes in populations;
- types of resources;
- changes in environments;
- science and technology in local challenges.

History and Nature of Science: All students should develop and understanding of

- science as a human endeavor.

Content Standards: Grades 5–8

Physical Science: All students should develop an understanding of

- properties and changes of properties in matter;
- motions and forces;
- transfer of energy.

Life Science: All student should develop and understanding of

- structure and function in living systems;
- reproduction and heredity;
- regulation and behavior;
- populations and ecosystems;
- diversity and adaptations of organisms.

Earth and Space Science: All students should develop an understanding of

- structure of the earth system;
- earth's history;
- earth in the solar system.

Science and Technology: All students should develop

- abilities of technological design;
- understandings about science and technology.

Science in Personal and Social Perspectives: All students should develop understanding of

- personal health;
- populations, resources, and environments;
- natural hazards;
- risks and benefits;
- science and technology in society.

History and Nature of Science: All students should develop understanding of

- science as a human endeavor;
- nature of science;
- history of science.

Content Standards: Grades 9–12

Physical Science: All students should develop an understanding of

- structure of atoms;
- chemical reactions;
- motions and forces;
- conservation of energy and increase in disorder;
- interactions of energy and matter.

Life Science: All students should develop an understanding of

- the cell;
- molecular basis of heredity;
- biological evolution;
- matter, energy, and organization in living systems;
- behavior of organisms.

Earth and Space Science: All student should develop an understanding of

- energy in the earth system;
- geochemical cycles;
- origin and evolution of the earth system;

♦ origin and evolution of the universe.

Science and Technology: All students should develop

♦ abilities of technological design;

♦ understandings about science and technology.

Science in Personal and Social Perspective: All students should develop an understanding of

♦ personal and community health;

♦ population growth;

♦ natural resources;

♦ environmental quality;

♦ natural and human-induced hazards;

♦ science and technology in local, national, and global challenges.

History and Nature of Science: All students should develop understanding of

♦ science as a human endeavor;

♦ nature of scientific knowledge;

♦ historical perspectives.

Science Education Program Standards

♦ All elements of the K–12 science program must be consistent with the other *National Science Education Standards* and with one another and developed within and across grade levels to meet a clearly stated set of goals.

♦ The program of study in science for all students should be developmentally appropriate, interesting, and relevant to students' lives; emphasize student understanding through inquiry; and be connected to all of the content standards.

♦ The science program should be coordinated with the mathematics program to enhance student use and understanding of mathematics in the study of science and to improve student understanding of mathematics.

♦ The K–12 science program must give students access to appropriate and sufficient resources, including quality teachers, time, materials, and equipment, adequate and safe space, and the community.

♦ All students in the K–12 science program must have equitable access to opportunities to achieve the *National Science Education Standards.*

- ◆ Schools must work as communities that encourage, support, and sustain teachers as they implement an effective science program.

Science Education System Standards

- ◆ Policies that influence the practice of science education must be congruent with the program, teaching, professional development, assessment, and content standards while allowing for adaptation to local circumstances.

- ◆ Policies that influence science education should be coordinated within and across agencies, institutions, and organizations.

- ◆ Policies need to be sustained over sufficient time to provide the continuity necessary to bring about the changes required by the *Standards.*

- ◆ Policies must be supported with resources.

- ◆ Science education policies must be equitable.

- ◆ All policy instruments must be reviewed for possible unintended effects on the classroom practice of science education.

- ◆ Responsible individuals must take the opportunity afforded by the standards-based reform movement to achieve the new vision of science education portrayed in the *Standards.*

Source: National Science Education Standards. (1996). Washington, DC: National Academy Press. Used with permission.

In keeping with the focus of this book, discussion in this chapter is limited to the Science Teaching Standards, the Assessment Standards, and the Content Standards.

The Science Teaching Standards

The Science Teaching Standards provide a general framework for instruction in PreK–12 science classrooms. These standards require science teachers to provide instruction in which students are not only active participants but also decision makers. Teachers are portrayed as facilitators of learning instead of disseminators of knowledge. Moreover, teachers are expected to be key decision makers about the school's science program. As a decision maker, the science teacher is positioned to make sure principals are aware of what resources are necessary for the science program.

The Assessment Standards

Once content is taught, teachers are responsible for making informed judgments concerning student learning. Because science tends to be a hands-on discipline, using a variety of assessment should be natural. Using multiple sources of data from assessments that are carefully aligned to the curriculum being taught to make assessment decisions allows students to demonstrate learning in a variety of ways and permits teachers to make more valid judgments.

The Content Standards

The Content Standards offer guidance to science teachers across the PreK–12 continuum. The first standard, and the only standard that spans the entire PreK–12 spectrum, sets the foundation for students to be active participants in science classes by having students learn how scientific inquiry is carried out, and then demonstrate those skills. Three subsets of content standards: elementary (K–4), middle school (grades 5–8), and high school (grades 9–12) describe broad instructional goals in the areas of physical, life, and earth and space science. Additionally, teachers are urged to include applications of science, particularly in the areas of technology and social issues. The final standard, History and Nature of Science, requires students to study how scientists throughout history have struggled to increase our knowledge of the natural world.

Science Curriculum
Across the PreK–12 Continuum

An examination of the *National Science Education Standards* provides valuable insight into the elements that make up the PreK–12 science curriculum. The obvious themes across the PreK–12 continuum are the study of physical, life, and earth and space science at all levels, the importance of technology to science, and the ongoing study of scientific inquiry itself. The following section provides some discussion of each of these themes.

Physical, Life, Earth, and Space Science

In physical science, students learn about inanimate objects on earth and the chemicals that comprise them. These include rocks, minerals, landforms (e.g., mountains, canyons), and the forces that can act on them (e.g., types of energy). These topics are presented in a developmental fashion. Elementary students are first introduced to objects with which they might already be familiar such as rocks and light bulbs. By middle school students should be learning how these objects change when different forces are applied such as heat changing water to water vapor. In high school, students begin examining and analyzing the components of the chemicals that comprise the physical world (e.g., atoms and molecules).

Life science introduces students to all of the living things on earth. Similar to the development of the physical science curriculum, the life sciences curriculum begins with life forms with which elementary children might be familiar. These could include dogs, cats, hamsters, and fish. Students at the elementary level are also commonly introduced to life cycles, particularly the life cycle of the frog and the butterfly. The final component of elementary life sciences is environment. Students learn where different organisms live and why.

By the middle grades, students concentrate their life science study on the structures that compose different organisms (e.g., skeleton, internal organs) and the relationships among different organisms. The high school life sciences curriculum mirrors the physical science curriculum. Just as the physical sciences curriculum examines the basic building blocks of physical objects, high school life science examines the basic building block of life—the cell. Other topics in the high school curriculum could include heredity, organization of living organisms, and behavior of organisms.

Earth and Space Science

The third major branch of the PreK–12 science curriculum allows the students to extend their views beyond the confines of earth. At the elementary level, students are introduced to the earth's nearest neighbors—the planets of our own solar system—as well as to basic objects in the sky such as stars and comets. These students also learn how the earth, sun, and the moon form the basis for months and seasons of the year. In the middle grades, students take a closer look at earth's history and the relationship of the earth to other objects in the sky. The high school curriculum usually includes the chemical and physical reactions that cause phenomena in space (e.g., sun spots) and also begins to explore theories about the origins of the earth and the universe.

The different content areas (physical science, life science, earth and space science) should be taught as interdependent disciplines as opposed to discrete disciplines that have no concepts or skills in common. One method of pulling these disciplines to together is found in the remaining themes: scientific inquiry and technology in science.

Scientific Inquiry

Scientific knowledge is advanced through the need to solve problems and to satisfy curiosity. Engaging students in inquiry helps students develop

- ◆ understanding of scientific concepts;
- ◆ an appreciation of "how we know" what we know in science;

- understanding of the nature of science;

- skills necessary to become independent inquirers about the natural world;

- the disposition to use the skills, abilities, and attitudes associated with science. (National Research Council, 1996, p. 105)

For science teachers and those who supervise them, it appears that students in PreK–12 science classes should become familiar with and be able to carry out a variety of processes to promote higher-level thinking skills.

The Supervisor's Scorecard

- Identifying questions that can be answered through scientific inquiry

- Designing and conducting scientific investigations

- Using appropriate tools and techniques to gather, analyze, and interpret data

- Developing descriptions, explanations, predictions, and models based on the evidence

- Thinking critically to identify the relationship between the evidence and the resulting explanations

---

Creativity can stir not only the imagination but also enhance learning through promoting the development of problem-posing and -solving skills. Creativity is a staple of promoting scientific inquiry, and teachers who promote creativity extend any single model of instruction across subject areas (see Chapter 4 and then subsequent supervision across subject matter chapters). Teachers can be coached as they practice and refine the use of creativity, and the supervisor can assist by providing feedback on how teachers employ techniques to enhance the development of creativity in students.

The cornerstone of any classroom observation, regardless of whether the observation is an informal or formal one, is that the quality of data collected in the observation determines the amount of sense the teacher and supervisor can make of the data during a post-observation conference. To enhance the collection of data relative to the use of creativity in the classroom, Figure 10.2, adapted from the work of Mohr (1999), can assist the supervisor and teacher to focus attention on the technique, creativity.

Figure 10.2. Tracking Creativity in Teaching

Instructional Technique	Teacher Behaviors to Support the Technique	Classroom Observation Notes
• Free your classroom of restraints based on time, material, and tasks	• Includes a variety of media for class projects including art supplies such as clay and paint. • Give options that address the same content but in different ways. • Vary the ways in which students work cooperatively and independently.	
• Model creativity. (A creative person is independent, takes risks, and is not afraid to make mistakes.)	• Show the value of making mistakes. • Model how to use the mistake as a learning opportunity.	
• Encourage and reward creative ideas.	• Recognize students who pursue creative ideas. • Create a penalty-free environment for students who "color outside the lines" or who make their pumpkin purple instead of orange. • Accept ideas that are outside the norm.	
• Withhold criticism while students are working on a project.	• Encourage students to evaluate their own ideas and solutions by posing questions to help students focus on an area of difficulty. For example, if a student is making a poster with tiny letters, you might ask, "How far away can the viewer read that?"	
• Choose activities that are appropriate and interesting.	• Capture and pique student interest by choosing local, personally relevant issues, such as local pollution or issues before the local government. • Use state and national education standards to help select activities for the age level of students.	
• Choose activities in which students must examine and relate to their surroundings.	• Help students learn to make scientific observations of things in the room or immediately outside the school.	

Instructional Technique	Teacher Behaviors to Support the Technique	Classroom Observation Notes
• Free your classroom of restraints based on time, material, and tasks	• Includes a variety of media for class projects including art supplies such as clay and paint. • Give options that address the same content but in different ways. • Vary the ways in which students work cooperatively and independently.	
• Model creativity. (A creative person is independent, takes risks, and is not afraid to make mistakes.)	• Show the value of making mistakes. • Model how to use the mistake as a learning opportunity.	
• Encourage questions and new ideas.	• Model asking questions that are open-ended, such as "Let's make a list of different sources of light." • Help students learn to phrase their own questions in an open-ended manner.	
• Accept ideas that look at problems from different angles.	• Turn the focus away from labeling responses right or wrong. • Accept divergent answers and explanations. If students find a solution that works, the teacher accepts it even if it's not the way the teacher thinks is best.	
• Set up a classroom environment that stimulates the senses.	• Use plants, animals, posters, and student work to enhance learning for students on all grade levels.	
• Use problem- and inquiry-based activities, especially problems with multiple solutions.	• Pose problems that require divergent thinking. For example, use earth and water to investigate what can be done to prevent flooding. Or ask, "How do you make a spool roll using only a rubber band and a paper clip?"	
• Ask students to make predictions.	• Encourages if-then thinking. For example, when a student predicts that dirt will settle to the bottom of a lake, ask, "If that is true, then what will happen in a river with a fast current?"	
• Ask students to elaborate on their ideas.	• Stretch their thinking by asking, "What evidence do you have to support that? What do you mean by _____?"	

Instructional Technique	Teacher Behaviors to Support the Technique	Classroom Observation Notes
• Free your classroom of restraints based on time, material, and tasks	• Includes a variety of media for class projects including art supplies such as clay and paint. • Give options that address the same content but in different ways. • Vary the ways in which students work cooperatively and independently.	
• Model creativity. (A creative person is independent, takes risks, and is not afraid to make mistakes.)	• Show the value of making mistakes. • Model how to use the mistake as a learning opportunity.	
• Empathize with the perspectives of others.	• Take all feelings into account by not discounting different perspectives as ill informed or irrelevant. • Help students who disagree to find common ground.	
• Brainstorm both as a class and in small groups.	• Promote flexibility through brainstorming sessions. • Start by using one word, for example, "bird." Put the word on the overhead and ask students what they think of when they hear that word. • Address misconceptions after assessing what students know. • Address misconceptions by introducing new ideas. • In small groups, ask students to begin a problem-solving activity by brainstorming issues to address when solving the problem or different ways to solve it.	
• Make concept maps with interconnecting relationship systems.	• Ask students to make as many con-nections as possible. • Ask students to think of phrases to label the lines that connect each con-cept.	

Instructional Technique	Teacher Behaviors to Support the Technique	Classroom Observation Notes
• Free your classroom of restraints based on time, material, and tasks	• Includes a variety of media for class projects including art supplies such as clay and paint. • Give options that address the same content but in different ways. • Vary the ways in which students work cooperatively and independently.	
• Model creativity. (A creative person is independent, takes risks, and is not afraid to make mistakes.)	• Show the value of making mistakes. • Model how to use the mistake as a learning opportunity.	
• Use wait time I and II.	• Practice using wait patterns. • Ask, "What would happen if there were no sun?" (wait time I) • Use student responses, "The flowers would die." • Then employ wait time II to give the student(s) a chance to elaborate.	
• Give more options for student presentations.	• Encourage students to communicate through singing, dancing, drawing, writing a poem, etc. • Foster accountability and self-reflection by engaging students in evaluating their own performance and the performance of others using specific criteria.	
• Guard against an over emphasis on correctness and perfectionism.	• Accept that logic does not solve everything. • Accept more than one answer or solution to any problem.	
• Listen to and acknowledge student ideas.	• Focus attention on student speakers. • Ensure that all have a chance to speak. • Acknowledge all contributions, without showing bias toward "best" answers.	

Instructional Technique	Teacher Behaviors to Support the Technique	Classroom Observation Notes
• Free your classroom of restraints based on time, material, and tasks	• Includes a variety of media for class projects including art supplies such as clay and paint. • Give options that address the same content but in different ways. • Vary the ways in which students work cooperatively and independently.	
• Model creativity. (A creative person is independent, takes risks, and is not afraid to make mistakes.)	• Show the value of making mistakes. • Model how to use the mistake as a learning opportunity.	
• Provide the medium or context, not just material to be memorized.	• Use questions that go beyond pat answers. • Provide activities that address the main concepts of the topic and/or the misconceptions revealed. • Refrain from requiring students to memorize unless that serves some purpose other than just knowing information.	

Source: Adapted from Mohr, Laura C. (1999). 20 Ways to Foster Creativity in Your Students. ENC Focus 6(2), 36–37. Reproduced with permission of Eisenhower National Clearinghouse; visit ENC Online (www.enc.org).

Technology in Science

When scientific breakthroughs occur, invariably technology is involved. Instruments such as microscopes, telescopes, and seismographs have assisted scientists to make discoveries that help cure disease, learn more about the stars, and more accurately predict natural disasters. Perhaps no technological innovation has had a greater effect on scientific inquiry than the computer. Massive amounts of data, previously too large to analyze meaningfully, can now be managed using computers. Computers have also been used to increase the effectiveness and accuracy of some scientific instruments. Applications of technology to science are equally important to knowledge of technology itself. Students need to be able to identify what types of questions can be addressed through existing technology and which questions cannot.

Human Development Theory and Implications for Science Instruction

A review of the *National Science Education Standards* reveals an important implication of human development theory to science instruction in PreK–12 classrooms. Piaget pointed out that children in early elementary school are at the preoperational stage. They are just beginning to be able to carry out mental processes concerning objects they cannot see. The NSES curriculum begins with objects with which children are familiar. They can go outside and see clouds, the sun, and rocks. As children become capable of concrete operations (upper elementary and middle school) the curriculum makes an important transition.

The abstract nature of scientific inquiry may seem beyond the reach of many elementary school students. Howe (1993) argues that children can learn science if instruction is firmly based the students' past experiences. Children's natural curiosity should be used as a catalyst for learning scientific inquiry. Activities such as nature hikes around the school yard can help stimulate scientific discussion. During the hike, students should be encouraged to describe what they observe while a recorder writes down the observations for later discussion in the classroom.

Hawkins (1965) described science in the elementary grades in terms of three phases: messing around, externally guided work, and transition from concrete perception to abstract conceptualization. In the messing around phase, students are allowed to freely examine objects selected to stimulate their imaginations. During the second phase, the teacher begins guiding students' learning toward the day's objective. The final phase occurs as the teacher assists the students in conceptualizing a theory based on their new learning.

The upper elementary and middle school content standards reflect students' developing skills with concrete operations. Instead of focusing study on objects such as clouds or rocks, students are now asked to study the relationships between these objects. For example, students at this level begin examining how physical objects such as soil and rivers interact with living things such as trees and animals to form an ecosystem. The high school curriculum makes a final transition from concrete to more abstract topics such as heredity and radioactive isotopes.

Instructional Strategies for the Science Classroom

As evidenced by the *National Science Education Standards*, science instruction should be hands-on in every sense of the word. Instead of just hearing about science, reading about science, and seeing science, students should also be *doing* science. Therefore, *active strategies* are needed in the science classroom. Effective teaching strategies for the science classroom include cooperative learning, inquiry, and simulations.

The Supervisor's Scorecard

According to the Council of State Science Coordinators (2002), good science teaching should be standards based and must incorporate building on past experiences of the learner, taking more time for the learner to assimilate the concepts, and fostering the use of more inquiry into the curriculum.

Great science teachers in PreK–12 classrooms

- Enjoy being with young people and believe that all students can learn.

- Serve as facilitators of learning, and are alert to student learning styles.

- Provide hands-on, inquiry-based activities.

- Maintain high expectations for all students.

- Use a variety of authentic assessment techniques that are embedded into the instructional fabric.

- Encourage students to utilize and evaluate research materials.

- Listen to students and encourage them to refine and extend their own thinking.

- Realize that true learning takes place when students reconcile new information with their existing knowledge, and structures classroom time to allow students the opportunity to integrate information.

Cooperative Learning in the Science Classroom

Science in the real world is a cooperative venture. Meaningful instruction in science classrooms should mirror this fact. Hartman and Glasgow (2002) argue that

> scientists seldom work in isolation; they usually require input and feedback from their peers to extend their own thinking. Often scientific enterprise is undertaken by teams; individuals cooperate with each other on a project, and teams cooperate with other teams. (p. 120)

Cooperative learning strategies provide opportunities to construct scientific knowledge together. Stone (2002) points out that "students become teachers to each of their teammates and also to the rest of their classmates" and that "students 'discuss science' during their in-class research… and help each other understand different points of view" (p. 130). A particularly effective cooperative learning strategy for the science classroom is the jigsaw technique.

Originally developed by Aronson (1978), jigsaw requires to students to extend basic cooperative learning skills through use of multiple group structures in the same learning activity. There are five steps to the jigsaw model of cooperative learning:

1. Introducing the jigsaw
2. Assigning heterogeneously grouped students to study teams
3. Assembling expert groups to study material
4. Experts teaching their study teams
5. Evaluating and recognizing team achievement (Gunter, Estes, & Schwab, 1999).

The jigsaw begins with the teacher explaining the curriculum to be covered in the exercise. Next, students are assigned to the teams in which they will work. After teams are formed, each student is assigned a specific responsibility. Following team formation, students are regrouped by responsibility. These new groups are called *expert groups* and provide the setting in which students will learn the skills necessary to their jobs for their teams. When the expert groups complete their work, teams are reassembled and begin their work. After all teams have completed their assigned tasks, teams share their work with one another. During this sharing time, the process can be evaluated.

In the science classroom, the jigsaw method has several benefits including increased student self-control, reduced intimidation among more introverted students, and improvement in students' reading abilities (Eppler & Huber, 1990). Through jigsaw, students gain expertise in a specific area of the curriculum and the opportunity to share that expertise with their peers to help solve a problem or to answer a question.

Inquiry in the Science Classroom

Perhaps no other teaching method is more natural for science instruction than Suchman's (1962) inquiry method. Suchman's steps of searching, data processing, discovery, verification closely parallel those of the scientific method. Figure 10.3 illustrates the relationship between the scientific method and Suchman's inquiry method.

Figure 10.3. Inquiry and the Scientific Method

Suchman's Inquiry Method	*The Scientific Method*
Searching: planned and controlled collection of data. Some phenomenon has been selected for observation.	*Observation:* Observe some aspect of the universe.
	Hypothesis: Invent a tentative description consistent with what you have observed and use the hypothesis to make a prediction.
Data Processing: Organization of data to discern possible pattern; data analysis.	*Testing the Prediction:* Data are collected through experiments, and students form conclusions based the data collected.
Discovery: The process of seeing how the data fit together.	*Modify:* Check for discrepancies between the hypothesis and the conclusions. Modify hypothesis based on discrepancies observed and repeat testing.
Verification: Checking conclusions and the process through which the conclusions were reached.	

Inquiry teaching is more conducive to helping students to think and to discuss more like scientists than the direct method of instruction. Yerrick (1998) examined one teacher's effort to transform a lower track science class from lecture-based to inquiry teaching. Results suggested that students' perceptions of the teacher as a major source of factual information inhibited efforts to become an inquiry-based class. Yerrick warns that inquiry-based science teaching goes against most students' preconceived notions concerning science instruction and learning.

Given the open-ended nature of inquiry, supervisors can help teachers by giving concrete feedback. Developed by the 2002 Council of State Science Supervisors (2002), the information in Figure 10.4 can assist the supervisor to collect data related specifically to the instructional method, inquiry.

Figure 10.4. Assessing Instruction for Inquiry

Characteristics of Teaching through Inquiry	*Evidence of Teaching through Inquiry*

Characteristics of teaching through inquiry:

- Teacher frequently asks more questions than imparts information.
- Levels of questions vary from knowledge to analysis.
- Facilitation strategies are used more than presenting strategies.
- Learners are probed to think more deeply about concepts.
- Communication with the teacher is two-way.
- Discourse among students is orchestrated.
- Students are challenged to accept and share responsibility for their own learning.
- Every student is encouraged to participate.
- Skills, attitudes and values of scientific inquiry are modeled by the teacher, including openness, curiosity, skepticism.
- Teachers use evidence gathered from student assessment data to guide their teaching.
- The setting is created for student work that is flexible and supportive of scientific inquiry.
- Tools, equipment, and technology is available to students.
- Diverse ideas and skills are respected.
- Collaboration among students is nurtured.

Simulations in the Science Classroom

The *National Science Education Standards* clearly expect science instruction to replicate real-world science as closely as possible. Despite these expectations, there is relatively little research on simulations in science classrooms (Hartman & Glasgow, 2002). One study, conducted by Francis and Byrne (1999), concluded simulation in astronomy and physics classes, "deepens student understanding and dramatically increases the level of classroom interaction" (p. 206). Perhaps the ultimate example of simulation in the science classroom occurs when students are allowed to leave the classroom and conduct scientific investigations *in the field*. Teachers can provide this opportunity through field trips or by creating an "outdoor" classroom.

Field Trips and Science Instruction

There is obviously a great deal of difference in studying swamps in the classroom and learning about swamps by visiting one. However, using field trips as a part of instruction requires more than just reserving transportation and sending home permission forms. Students need to master skills and knowledge prerequisite to successfully completing the activities scheduled for the field trip prior to leaving the classroom (Finley, 1991). If a museum is involved, contact the museum staff ahead of the trip and be sure students make connect the field trip to their class work.

Outdoor Classrooms and Science Instruction

For some, the ultimate site for science learning is an outdoor classroom. An outdoor classroom is a site, usually on or near the school yard, which is set aside for science study. Outdoor classrooms give students a place where experiments in physical and life science can be conducted in a natural setting. Much information on preparing an outdoor classroom is available on the Internet.

The Supervisor in the Science Classroom

Science classrooms offer diverse challenges to the principals who supervise teachers working in them. The following "Look Fors" (Figure 10.5) developed by Dr. James V. Foran et al. (2000) from the Maryland State Department of Education offer guidance for high school principals supervising in biology classes.

Figure 10.5. Administrator "Look Fors" in Biology

Rather than random lesson planning in biology or simply following the table of contents of a textbook...

> Teachers plan with the Core Learning Goals, Expectations, Indicators, and Assessment Limits in mind. Assessment Limits are extremely important because they prescribe the nonnegotiable topics of each concept that must be covered to ensure that students have been taught the material that will be tested. Teachers are invited to go as far beyond the Assessment Limits as time, their level of expertise, and the ability levels of the students they are teaching will allow.

Rather than planning lessons that teach biological concepts as ends unto themselves...

> Teachers plan lessons using the "5E" format–Engagement, Exploration, Explanation, Extension, and Evaluation.

Rather than lecturing...

> Teachers use a variety of hands-on and minds-on instructional strategies to make the subject of biology come alive.

Rather than regarding students as passive learners...

> Teachers engage students as biologists. This involves preparing lessons that incorporate reading, writing, and/or oral communication about biology as often as possible.

Rather than presenting biological concepts in isolation...

> Teachers weave together the concepts of biology and the skills and processes of science so that students understand that the processes of science are equally as important as the content.

Rather than presenting the content of biology in isolation...

> Teachers involve the students in real-world applications of biological concepts.

Rather than discussing biology in isolation...

> Teachers help students make connections with prior scientific knowledge as well as between science and other content areas.

Rather than merely talking about the technology of modern science...

> Teachers frequently incorporate technology into classroom and laboratory activities. In cases where the equipment is too expensive to put into the hands of all students, teachers may demonstrate its use for the students; in cases where the equipment is too sophisticated

for use in a high school classroom, the teacher may demonstrate its use via a video. In all cases, technology, including use of the Internet, must be given much more than cursory attention in the study of biology.

Rather than presenting biological information as a series of unrelated, disjointed facts…

Teachers present the concepts of biology as a unified body of knowledge.

Rather than always following cookbook-type lab exercises…

Students frequently have the opportunity to design and conduct their own biology investigations.

Rather than assessing recall or the students' ability to regurgitate facts…

Teachers invite students to interact with and analyze real data, determine the relevance of real data to authentic situations, contemplate scientific evidence, make predictions, form their own conclusions, judge the reasonableness of the conclusions of other scientists, map out next steps in scientific investigations, etc.

Rather than giving assignments to reinforce facts…

Teachers design assignments that require students to discover, probe, explore the concepts of biology and/or apply biological concepts and information to the real world in which they live.

Rather than assessing only at the end of a unit…

Teachers use ongoing, periodic, appropriate, formative assessments to gauge student learning and to make adjustments in instruction.

Rather than assessing discrete facts…

Teachers assess the understanding and interrelationship of biological concepts.

Source: Dr. James V. Foran et al. (2000). Maryland State Department of Education. Retrieved November 25, 2003 from http://www.msde.state.md.us/hsimprovement/ administratorlookfors.html. Used with permission.

The *National Science Education Standards* can provide a framework for guiding observations in all science classrooms. These standards portray science instruction as inquiry based and student centered. Data collection in the science classroom should be able answer these questions:

♦ Are students encouraged to *formulate* as well as conduct scientific investigations?

- Does the teacher ensure that prerequisite skills such as knowing how to use equipment safely and properly are in place?

- Does the teacher check to see if students have the necessary reading and math skills necessary to conduct scientific inquiry?

- Are classroom activities textbook and worksheet driven?

- Are the school's technology resources in evidence in science instruction?

- Does the teacher provide opportunities for students to study science in natural settings?

- Does the teacher link new topics to experiences and places familiar to the students?

These questions can be answered without the benefit of a science background. Carefully selected data concerning teacher and student behavior can assist the principal and science teacher in making informed judgments about instruction in the science classroom.

Just as the science classroom should be an environment that encourages student inquiry and learning, it should also be a place where teacher learning and inquiry occur. Data that accurately portray teacher and student behavior can provide meaningful fodder for discussion between teacher and principal. In turn, teacher–principal discussions based on jointly analyzed classroom data can build the foundation for future learning. In essence, science teachers and principals can use the scientific method of data collection and draw conclusions based on the data.

Suggested Readings

Aronson, E. (1978). *The jigsaw classroom.* Beverly Hills, CA: Sage.

Bourne, B. (Ed.). (2000). *Taking inquiry outdoors: Reading, writing, and science beyond the classroom walls.* Portland, ME: Stenhouse.

Hartman, H. J., & Glasgow, N. A. (2002). *Tips for the science teacher: Research-based strategies to help students learn.* Thousand Oaks, CA: Corwin Press.

Howe, A. C. (1993). Science in early childhood education. In B. Spodek (Ed.), *Handbook of research on the education of young children* (pp. 225–235). New York: MacMillan.

Yerrick, R. (1998). Reconstructing classroom facts: Transforming lower-track science classrooms. *Journal of Science Teacher Education, 9*(2), 241–270.

11

Ready, Set, Go

The work of the principal supervising the instructional program is one in which there are many complexities. The press for accountability at the hub of the labor of meeting adequate yearly progress and the constant demands of the work outside of the realm of instruction often leaves little time for the work that principals must do to ensure learning for teachers and students. These pressures are perennial, and they will continually present challenges and opportunities for the principal.

As indicated in Chapter 1, this book covers in depth the supervision of four core subjects: mathematics, English/language arts, social studies, and science. However, the supervisory tools along with the concepts presented about multiple intelligences, brain-based learning, learning styles, the characteristics of learners across grades PreK–12, and select instructional strategies (cooperative learning, Socratic Seminar, inquiry) to deliver the curriculum can be applied in other content areas (foreign language, fine arts, physical education).

It was not our intent to marginalize other content areas by our coverage of supervision in select subjects. We made a purposeful decision to focus on content areas that have served as the bedrock of the instructional program in PreK–12 schools, and we have confidence that principals will be able to see the applicability of what we have presented across the content areas not covered in this book.

Principals can apply the tools and resources presented in this book to help lead schools toward improved instruction through focused supervision that aligns with content, curriculum, and instructional strategies that are appropriate for students' developmental stages. We hope that this book can serve to further the understanding of supervising teachers across various content areas and to promote thinking about the absolute need to provide collaborative opportunities in the work needed to improve student learning. Through working with teachers in their classrooms, supervisors can gain insight into the complexities of teaching and learning while developing empathy for the work teachers do on a daily basis. However, a book can never be enough unless the principal takes concepts beyond the print to action.

Taking Action

To take action across not only supervising the subject areas presented in this book but also in other areas, principals must embrace a vision that all teachers want to be effective and that by nurturing and encouraging teachers, students will benefit from these efforts. The message of this book is that

> quality teaching and knowledge about instruction should be a part of the vision for student achievement. Instructional leadership involves knowing what good teaching is and how good teaching leads to student learning. Building a vision for student success and instructional leadership is an ongoing reflective process, and building the vision among the members of the school community is an iterative process that begins with the instructional leader looking within for the core values and beliefs that motivate her to act on these values and beliefs. The effective principal also looks to the school community to engage all stakeholders in developing the vision. The vision drives all actions and allocation of resources. Instructional leaders protect the vision, leading people toward the end goal. (Zepeda, 2003b)

For principals to be effective supervisors and to promote the type of supervision that enhances growth and development, they first must be able to identify their core beliefs about what is "good" teaching. Although this might appear to be an academic exercise, without this awareness of beliefs and values, principals will find it difficult to engage in meaningful discussions with teachers. Moreover, without this awareness, it will be difficult to lead teachers in exploring their own beliefs about teaching and learning. The following questions can serve to guide principals and other administrative team members in the process of looking individually and then collectively at beliefs about teaching and learning.

- What do I stand for?
- What is my personal vision about teaching, students, and achievement?
- What does good teaching look like?
- What separates good teaching from excellent teaching, mediocre teaching?
- What types of support do teachers need?
- What types of teaching do students need to learn?
- Can all children learn?

Source: Zepeda (2003b).

The answers to these questions can help the principal not only communicate expectations for learning and teaching, but more importantly, these answers can also lead the principal in framing discussions with teachers. To complete the examination of core beliefs about teaching and learning, teachers have to be part of the process. Principals need to engage their teachers in the discussion to develop a system-wide set of core beliefs. This process takes time, and the principal needs to ensure that teachers have the time to storm and norm with one another. These types of discussions must occur over time so that beliefs and practices can evolve.

The culture and the climate of the school will either encourage or stifle open exchanges. Trust and a fault-free environment must be established and maintained. Of course, such discussions will sometimes become "messy" and fraught with lively and charged disagreement. This is the beauty of the process. The astute principal recognizes the inevitable—there are no absolutes given the contextualized nature of leading, learning, teaching, and the interaction of these with variables that make each school unique.

Recognizing the Inevitable

Schools are not static. There is an ebb and flow in which variables interact with one another constantly changing the landscape of learning and teaching; therefore, absolutes do not exist. Principals, like teachers, vary in their knowledge of instructional strategies with which they are familiar. Teachers often teach different grade levels in subjects in which they are certified. Some teachers are assigned to teach in areas that fall outside of their major in which they were certified as many states have provisions in which teachers can teach subject areas as long as they have a minimum amount of coursework. Teachers often change grade levels, encountering new curriculum and children at different levels of development. Some teachers are alternatively certified and others have had delays in which they entered teaching after being certified.

Schools are staffed with teachers whose experiences span the career continuum from beginning to veteran status. The educational levels of teachers vary as well with some teachers holding advanced degrees, and the recency of advanced coursework varies as well. The amount and sophistication of staff development and personal and professional learning opportunities in which teachers engage vary from teacher to teacher and school to school.

All of this serves to emphasize that teachers vary in their skills and knowledge; they vary in their comfort levels to learn new practices; and that they vary in their willingness to change instructional practices.

Becoming Opportunistic Learners

Principals answer the call to supervisory leadership by working with teachers, capitalizing on their expertise, and coaching them toward higher levels of competence in the application and refinement of instructional strategies that enhance student learning given the context in which instruction unfolds. Principals need to become opportunistic, seeking to learn as much as possible about teaching and learning across the grade levels and subject areas that span the schools in which they lead. Teachers need to have confidence in their principals' knowledge about content and appropriate instruction. Without this requisite knowledge, credibility diminishes.

Principals can learn a great deal about teaching by attending seminars and other types of staff development, enrolling in graduate coursework, consulting with central office subject matter experts, and observing teachers teach. Principals are in a prime position to observe a variety of instruction, and every classroom observation is a learning opportunity for both the teacher and the principal. Principals who are "out and about," engaging in classroom observations are also in a position to encourage teachers who also want to learn about teaching and learning to observe one another, to engage in conversations about their teaching, and to reflect on the results of their efforts.

Principals look for purposeful ways to connect with teachers. Principals also look for ways to make learning opportunities available to teachers, and to connect these learning opportunities so that learning is seamless. Consider the range of learning opportunities that principals can offer to teachers and note the linkages that are present across opportunities (Figure 11.1).

Figure 11.1. Linking Supervisory and Professional Development Learning Opportunities

Professional Development and Supervisory Opportunities	How These Opportunities Are Linked
Peer Coaching	Numerous peer coaches serve as mentors, coaching teachers through direct classroom observation that includes both pre- and post-observation conferences.
Mentoring and Induction	The induction program includes mentoring, peer coaching, and study groups.

Study Groups	Teachers form study groups and examine instructional issues; groups may read common materials; some teachers are involved in peer coaching; some teachers extend study group activities with teacher-directed action research.
Portfolio Development	Action research teams are developing portfolios to track changes in practice.
Action Research Teams	Groups of teachers conduct action research on classroom practices and stay with a problem of practice for an extended period.

Source: Zepeda (2003a). Used with permission.

Focusing and Refocusing on Supervision

The primary purpose of this book is to promote effective supervisory practices. In addition to assisting teachers to grow and to develop, instructional supervision can serve as a means to promote school improvement. Supervisory efforts supporting, "All programs—staff development, mentoring, induction, peer coaching—can assist the principal focus the attention of the school on improvement" (Zepeda, 2004, p. 131). Efforts that promote the development of school personnel need to work in tandem with the efforts of improvement, no matter how small or big. Supervision and other forms of professional development will yield more positive results if they focus teachers and schools toward student learning and achievement. To this end, efforts need to be learner-centered for students, teachers, and principals to support the school as a learning community. We ask the principal to consider framing supervisory and professional development on the principles advocated in 1999 by the National Partnership for Excellence and Accountability in Teaching (Figure 11.2).

Figure 11.2. Revisioning Professional Development

♦ The content of professional development focuses on what students are to learn and how to address the different problems students may have in learning the material.

♦ Professional development should be based on analyses of the differences between (a) actual student performance and (b) goals and standards for student learning.

♦ Professional development should involve teachers in identifying what they need to learn and in developing the learning experiences in which they will be involved.

♦ Professional development should be primarily school-based and built into the day-to-day work of teaching.

♦ Most professional development should be organized around collaborative problem solving.

♦ Professional development should be continuous and ongoing, involving follow-up and support for further learning—including support from sources external to the school that can provide necessary resources and new perspectives.

♦ Professional development should incorporate evaluation of multiple sources of information on (a) outcomes for students and (b) the instruction and other processes involved in implementing lessons learned through professional development.

♦ Professional development should provide opportunities to understand the theory underlying the knowledge and skills being learned.

♦ Professional development should be connected to a comprehensive change process focused on improving student learning.

Source: *Revisioning Professional Development: What Learner-Centered Professional Development Looks Like.* National Partnership for Excellence and Accountability in Teaching (1999, p. 3). http://www.nsdc.org/NPEAT213.pdf

Instructional supervision, regardless of its form must become relevant to the instructional lives of teachers, be replete with feedback, support reflection, and facilitate the transfer of new skills into practice. Given the intents of instructional supervision (see Chapter 2), principals actively seek out differentiated methods of working with teachers.

Parting Thoughts

Supervising instruction is a daunting task because it takes time, commitment, and command of a range of skills. Learning these skills takes practice and then more practice so that refinements can be made. The supervision of instruction, however, also requires a broader view of what occurs in classrooms and the types of feedback given during a post-observation conference.

The Panasonic Foundation works with large urban school systems in an effort to help them create "systems of equity and quality in which all students are educated to high levels—in every school, in every classroom, and regardless of background." To bring teaching and learning to the forefront of the school, the essential responsibilities of school leaders are

♦ to clarify and promote the core value that *all* students can and will learn at high levels;

- to ensure a culture and climate of care, commitment, and continuous improvement;

- to establish and promote rigorous learning standards for *all* students based on the core value of *all means all;*

- to establish clear and rigorous expectations for, and to monitor the performance of, all system personnel toward all students achieving rigorous learning standards;

- to ensure that all system personnel have the ongoing professional learning necessary to meet the high performance expectations;

- to ensure that fiscal and other resources are provided to *all* schools so that they have what they need to help *all* students achieve standards;

- to implement a shared-accountability system that holds students, staff, and the system itself accountable for *all* students meeting rigorous standards;

- to engage in advocacy, coalitions, and other significant relationships at the local, state, and national levels so that the system can achieve *all means all.*

Source: Panasonic Foundation. (n.d.). http://www.panasonic.com/MECA/foundation/esspar.html Used with permission.

Perhaps through the process of learning about teaching, principals can broaden their view and assist teachers in expanding their range of skills. Teachers need principals who are committed to learning and leading so that *all* can learn.

References

Acheson, K. A., & Gall, M. D. (1997). *Techniques in the clinical supervision of teachers: Preservice and inservice applications* (4th ed.). White Plains, NY: Longman Publishers.

Acheson, K. A., & Gall, M .D. (2002). *Clinical supervision and teacher development: Preservice and inservice applications,* 5th ed. San Francisco: Jossey-Bass.

Adelman, N. E., Walking Eagle, K. P., & Hargreaves, A. (1997). Framing the cases: Time for change. In N. E. Adelman, K. P. Walking Eagle, & A. Hargreaves (Eds.), *Racing with the clock: Making time for teaching and learning in school reform* (pp. 1–7). New York: Teachers College Press.

Armstrong, D. G. (2003). *Curriculum today.* Upper Saddle River, NJ: Merrill Prentice Hall.

Aronson, E. (1978). *The jigsaw classroom.* Beverly Hills, CA: Sage Publications.

Avery, C. S. (1990). Learning to research/researching to learn. In M. W. Olson (Ed.), *Opening the door to classroom research* (pp. 32–44). Newark: International Reading Association.

Baddeley, A. (1986). *Working memory.* Oxford: Oxford University Press.

Ball, W. H., & Brewer, P. F. (1996). Socratic seminars. In R. L. Canady & M. D. Rettig (Eds.), *Teaching in the block: Strategies for engaging active learners* (pp. 29–64). Larchmont, NY: Eye on Education.

Bandura, A. (1969). *Principles of behavior modification.* New York: Holt, Rinehart, and Winston.

Bandura, A. (1977). *Social learning theory.* Englewood Cliffs, NJ: Prentice Hall.

Barber, B. L., Eccles, J. S., & Stone, M. R. (2001). Whatever happened to the jock, the brain, and the princess? Young adult pathways linked to adolescent activity involvement and social identity. *Journal of Adolescent Research, 16*(5), 429–455.

Barnett-Clark, C., & Ramirez, A. (Eds.). (2003). *Number sense and operations in the primary grades: Hard to teach and hard to learn?* Portsmouth, NH: Heinemann.

Barr, R., Barth, J., & Shermis, S. S. (1978). *The nature of the social studies.* Palm Springs, CA: ETC Publications.

Benjamin, A. (2002). *Differentiated instruction: A guide for middle and high school teachers.* Larchmont, NY: Eye On Education.

Benson, G. D., & Hunter, W. J. (1992). Chaos theory: No strange attractor in teacher education. *Action in Teacher Education 14*(4), 61–67.

Berk, L. A. (2002). *Infants, children, and adolescents* (4th ed.). Boston: Allyn & Bacon.

Berninger, V. W., & Richards, T. L. (2002). *Brain literacy for educators and psychologists.* Amsterdam: Academic Press.

Black, S. (2003, December). Engaging the disengaged: Research shows why some students are immersed in learning while others are indifferent. *American School Board Journal.* Retrieved December 5, 2003, from http://www.asbj.com/current/research.html

Blumberg, A. (1980). *Supervisors and teachers: A private cold war* (2nd ed.). Berkley, CA: McCutchan.

Bottoms, G. (n.d.). What school principals need to know about curriculum and instruction. Retrieved October 17, 2003, from http://www.sreb.org/programs/hstw/publications/pubs/WhatSchoolPrincipalsNeedtoKnow.pdf

Broderick, P. C., & Blewitt, P. (2003). *The life span: Human development for helping professionals.* Upper Saddle River, NJ: Merrill Prentice Hall.

Brooks-Gunn, J., & Warren, M. P. (1989). Biological and social contributions to negative affect in young adolescent girls. *Child Development, 60*(3), 40–55.

Brown, B. L. (1997). *Portfolio assessment: Missing link in student evaluation.* Columbus, OH: ERIC Clearinghouse on Adult, Career, and Vocational Education. (ERIC Document Reproduction Service No. ED 414 447)

Bruer, J. T. (1998). Brain science, brain fiction. *Educational Leadership, 56*(3), 14–19.

Bruno, J. (1988). An experimental investigation of the relationships between and among hemispheric processing, learning style preferences, instructional strategies, academic achievement, and attitudes of developmental mathematics students in an urban technical college. St. John's University. *Dissertation Abstracts International, 49*(08A), 2137.

Butler, G. E., McKie, M., & Ratcliffe, S. G. (1990). The cyclical nature of prepubertal growth. *Annals of Human Biology, 17*(3), 177–198.

Caine, R. N., & Caine, G. (1997). *Education on the edge of possibility.* Alexandria, VA: Association for Supervision and Curriculum Development.

Canady, R. L., & Rettig, M. D. (1995). *Block scheduling: A catalyst for change in high schools.* Larchmont, NY: Eye On Education.

Candler, L. (2003). *Cooperative learning checklist.* Retrieved November 13, 2003, from http://home.att.net/~clnetwork/co-op/trshoot.pdf

Carpenter, T. P., Franke, M. L., & Levi, L. (2003). *Thinking mathematically: Integrating arithmetic & algebra in elementary school.* Portsmouth, NH: Heinemann.

Casey, B. J., Giedd, J. N., & Thomas, K. M. (2000). Structural and functional brain development and its relation to cognitive development. *Biological Psychology, 54*(1) 241–257.

Charlesworth, R. (2004). *Understanding child development* (6th ed.). Clifton Park, NY: Thomson Learning.

Chugani, H. T. (1999). PET scanning studies of human brain development and plasticity. *Developmental neuropsychology, 16*(3), 379–381.

Clark, M. M. (1984). Literacy at home and at school: Insights from a study of young, fluent readers. In H. Goelman, A. Oberg, & F. Smith (Eds.), *Awakening to literacy* (pp. 153–167). Exeter, NH: Heinemann.

Clay, M. M. (1979). *Reading: The patterning of complex behavior.* Exeter, NH: Heinemann.

Cody, C. (1983). Learning styles, including hemispheric dominance: A comparative study of average, gifted, and highly gifted students in grades five through twelve. (Doctoral Dissertation, Temple University, 1983). *Dissertation Abstracts International, 44,* 1631–6A.

Cogan, M. (1973). *Clinical supervision.* Boston: Houghton-Mifflin.

Combs, M. (1996). *Developing competent readers and writers in the primary grades.* Englewood Cliffs, NJ: Merrill.

Costa, A. L., & Garmston, R. J. (1994). *Cognitive coaching: Foundation for renaissance schools.* Norwood, MA: Christopher-Gordon.

Council of State Science Supervisors. (2002). *Assessing Instruction for Inquiry: A Workshop.* Retrieved November 10, 2003, from http://www.inquiryscience.com/documents/InstructionW.pdf

Courtright, R. D. (2003). *Socratic inquiry and seminar teaching.* Retrieved November 24, 2003, from http://home.comcast.net/~dededye1/SOCRATICINQUIRYANDSEMINAR.DOC

Cowan, P. A. (1978). *Piaget with feeling: Cognitive social, and emotional dimensions.* New York: Holt, Rinehart, & Winston.

Cox, C. (1999). *Teaching language arts: A student- and response-centered approach* (3rd ed.). Boston: Allyn & Bacon.

D'Arcangelo, M. (1998). The brains behind the brain. *Educational Leadership, 56*(3), 20–25.

Darling-Hammond, L. (1995). Restructuring schools for student success. *Daedalus, 12*(4), 153–156.

DeMott, J. (1999). Seven steps to articulation success. *High School Magazine, 6*(4), 22–24.

Dewey, J. W. (1929). *Sources of science education.* New York: Liverisht.

Dewey, J. W. (1938). *Education and experience.* New York: Collier MacMillan.

Dick, B. (1999). *What is action research?* Retrieved October 22, 2003, from http://www.scu.edu.au/schools/gcm/ar/whatisar.html

Division of Science Resources Statistics. (2002). *Scientists, engineers, and technicians in the United States: 1998.* Washington, DC: National Science Foundation. Retrieved September 1, 2003, from www.nsf.gov/sbe/srs/nsf02313/pdf/secta.pdf

Dorsch, N. G. (1998). *Community, collaboration, and collegiality in school reform: An odyssey toward connections.* Albany, NY: State University of New York Press.

Dunn, R., Beaudry, J. S., & Klavas, A. (1989). Survey of research on learning styles. *Educational Leadership, 46*(6), 50–58.

Dunn, R., & Dunn, K. (1978). *Teaching students through their individual learning styles: A practical approach.* Reston, VA: Reston Publishing Company.

Durkin, D. (1966). *Children who read early.* New York: Teachers College Press.

Elkind, D. (1984). *All grown up and no place to go.* Reading, MA: Addison-Wesley.

Elkjaer, B. (1999). In search of a social learning theory. In M. Easterby-Smith, J. Burgoyne, & L. Araujo (Eds.), *Organizational learning and the learning organization: Developments in theory and practice* (pp.75–91). Thousand Oaks, CA: Sage.

Ellington, A. J. (2003). A meta-analysis of the effects of calculators on students' achievement and attitude levels in precollege mathematics classes. *Journal for Research in Mathematics Education, 34*(5), 433–463.

Ellis, A. K. (2004). *Exemplars of curriculum theory.* Larchmont, NY: Eye On Education.

English, F. (1984). Curriculum mapping and management. In B. D. Sattes (Ed.), *Promoting school excellence through the application of effective schools research: Summary and proceedings of a 1984 regional exchange workshop.* (ERIC Document Reproduction Service No. ED251972).

Eppler, R., & Huber, G. L. (1990). Wissenswert im Team: Empirische Untersuchung von Effekten des Gruppen-Puzzles [Acquisition of knowledge in teams: An empirical study of the effects of the jigsaw technique]. *Psychologie in Erziehunmg und Unterricht, 37*(1), 172–178.

Erikson, E. H. (1997). *The life cycle completed.* New York: Norton.

Erickson, L. (2001). Stirring the head, heart, and soul: Redefining curriculum and instruction. Thousand Oaks, CA: Corwin Press.

Eson, M. E., & Wolmsky, S. A. (1980). Promoting cognitive and psycholinguist development. In M. Johnson (Ed.), *Toward adolescence: The middle school years. 79th Yearbook of the National Society or the Study of Education. Part One.* Chicago: University of Chicago Press.

Fenwick, L. T., & Pierce, M. C. (2001). Is the principal an endangered species? *Principal, 89*(4), 1–6.

Feuerstein, R. (1980). *Instrumental enrichment: An intervention program for cognitive modifiability.* Glenview, IL: Scott-Foresman Lifelong Learning Division.

Finley, F. N. (1991). Why students have trouble learning from science texts. In C. M. Santa & D. E. Alvermann (Eds.), *Science learning: Processes and implications* (pp. 22–27). Newark, DE: International Reading Association.

Favell, J. H., Miller, P. H., & Miller, S. A. (1993). *Cognitive development* (3rd ed.). Upper Saddle River, NJ: Prentice Hall.

Foran, J.V., Schultz, G., Kaniecki, L., Yienger, L, & Newberry, G. (2000). *Look Fors*. The High School Improvement Program Technical Assistance Group at the Maryland State Department of Education. Retrieved November 25, 2003, from http://www.msde.state.md.us/hsimprovement/administrator lookfors.html

Fosnot, C. (1996). Constructivism: A psychological theory of learning. In C. Fosnot (Ed.), *Constructivism: Theory, perspectives, and practice* (pp.8–33). New York: Teachers College Press.

Francis, P. J., & Byrne, A. P. (1999). Using role-playing exercises in teaching undergraduate astronomy and physics. *Publications of the Astronomical Society of Australia, 16*(2), 206–211.

Frandsen, B. (2003). Participation rubric for unit development. Austin, TX: St. Edward's University, Center for Teaching Excellence. Retrieved January 5, 2003, from http://www.stedwards.edu/cte/resources/grub.htm

Fuligni, A. J., Eccles, J. S., Barber, B. L., & Clements, P. (2001). Early adolescent peer orientation and adjustment during high school. *Developmental Psychology, 37*(1), 28–36.

Gagnon, G. W., & Collay, M. (2001). *Constructivist learning design*. Retrieved January 7, 2001, from http://www.prainbow.com/cld/cldp.html

Gardner, H. (n.d.). Tapping into multiple intelligences. Retrieved October 1, 2003, from http://www.thirteen.org/edonline/concept2class/month1/

Gardner, H. (1982). *Developmental psychology* (2nd ed.). Boston: Little, Brown.

Gardner, H. (1993). *Frames of mind: The theory of multiple intelligences*. New York: Basic Books.

Gardner, H. (1999). *Intelligence reframed: Multiple intelligences for the 21st Century*. New York: Basic Books.

Gathercole, S. E. (1998). The development of memory. *Journal of Child Psychology and Psychiatry, 39*(1), 3–27.

George, P. S., & Alexander, W. M. (1993). *The exemplary middle school* (2nd ed.). Fort Worth, TX: Harcourt Brace Jovanovich.

Gingiss, P. L. (1993). Peer coaching: Building collegial support for using innovative health programs. *Journal of School Health, 63*(2), 79–85.

Glatthorn A. A. (1984). *Differentiated supervision*. Alexandra, VA: Association for Supervision and Curriculum.

Glatthorn, A. A. (1990). *Supervisory leadership: Introduction to instructional supervision*. New York: HarperCollins.

Glatthorn. A. A. (1997). *Differentiated supervision* (2nd ed.). Alexandria, VA: Association for Supervision and Curriculum Development.

Glickman, C. D. (1990). *Supervision of instruction: A development approach* (2nd ed.). Boston: Allyn & Bacon.

Glickman, C. D. (1981). *Developmental supervision: Alternative practices for helping teachers improve instruction*. Alexandria, VA: Association for Supervision and Curriculum Development.

Glickman, C. D. (1985). *Supervision of instruction: A developmental approach*. Boston: Allyn & Bacon.

Goldsberry, L. F. (1998). Teacher involvement in supervision. In G. R. Firth & E. F. Pajak (Eds.), *Handbook of research on school supervision* (pp. 428–462). New York: Simon & Schuster Macmillan.

Grady, M. P. (1998). *Qualitative and action research: A practitioner handbook*. Bloomington, ID: Phi Delta Kappa.

Gray, J. A. (1990). Brain systems that mediate both emotion and cognition. *Cognition and Emotion, 4,* 270–288.

Gunter, M. A., Estes, T. H., & Schwab, J. (1999). *Instruction: A models approach* (3rd ed.). Needham Heights, MA: Allyn & Bacon.

Harter, S. (1996). Developmental changes in self-understanding across the 5 to 7 shift. In A. J. Sameroff, & M. M. Haith (Eds.), *The five to seven year shift* (pp. 207–236). Chicago: University of Chicago Press.

Hartman, H. J., & Glasgow, N. A. (2002). *Tips for the science teacher: Research-based strategies to help students learn*. Thousand Oaks, CA: Corwin Press.

Hawkins, D. (1965). Messing about in science. *Science and Children, 2*(5), 5–9.

Heibert, E. H., & Colt, J. (1989). Patterns of literature-based reading instruction. *The Reading Teacher, 43*(1), 14–20.

Henson, K. T. (1995). *Curriculum development for education reform*. New York: HarperCollins College Publishers.

Hertzberg, H. W. (1981). *Social studies reform: 1880–1980*. Boulder, CO: Social Science Education Consortium.

Howe, A. C. (1993). Science in early childhood education. In B. Spodek (Ed.), *Handbook of research on the education of young children* (pp. 225–235). New York: MacMillan.

Ingersoll, R. (1995). *Teacher supply, teacher qualifications, and teacher turnover.* (NCES Report No. 95–744). Washington, DC: United States Department of Education.

International Reading Association and National Council of Teachers of English. (1996). *Standards for the English language arts.* Urbana, IL: National Council of Teachers of English and Newark, DE: International Reading Association. Author.

Jensen, E. (1998). *Teaching with the brain in mind.* Alexandria, VA: Association for Supervision and Curriculum Development.

Johnson, S. M. (1990). *Teachers at work.* New York: Basic Books.

Johnson, D. W., & Johnson, R. T. (1990). Social skills for successful group work. *Educational Leadership, 47*(4), 29–33.

Johnson, D. W., & Johnson, R. T. (1994). Learning together. In S. Sharan (Ed.), *Handbook of cooperative learning methods* (pp. 51–65). Westport, CT: Greenwood Press.

Johnson, D. W., Johnson, R. T., & Smith, K. (1991). *Active learning: Cooperation in the college classroom.* Edina, MN: Interaction Book Company.

Johnston, R., & Usher, R. (1997). Retheorizing experience: Adult learning in contemporary social practices. *Studies in the Education of Adults, 29*(2), 137–154. Retrieved October 4, 1999, from http://www.galib.uga.edu

Jorgenson, O. (2003). Brain scam? Why educators should be careful about embracing brain research. *The Educational Forum, 67*(4), 364–369.

Joyce, B., & Showers, B. (1982). The coaching of teaching. *Educational Leadership, 40*(1), 4–11.

Joyce, B., & Showers, B. (1981). Transfer of learning: The contribution of "coaching." *Boston University Journal of Education, 163*(2), 163–172.

Joyce, B., & Showers, B. (1995). *Student achievement through staff development: Fundamentals of school renewal* (2nd ed.). White Plains: Longman Publishers.

Joyce, B., & Weil, M. (1996). *Models of teaching* (5th ed.). Boston: Allyn & Bacon.

Jung, K. (1927). *The theory of psychological type.* Princeton, NJ: Princeton University Press.

Kagan, S. (1992). *Cooperative learning.* San Juan Capistrano, CA: Resources for Teachers.

Kagan, S. (1995). Group grades miss the mark. *Educational Leadership, 5*(8), 68–71.

Kaltsounis, T. (1979). *Teaching social studies in elementary school: The basics for citizenship.* Englewood Cliffs, NJ: Prentice-Hall.

Kato, Y., Kamii, C., Ozaki, K., & Nagahiro, M. (2002). Young children's representations of groups of objects: The relationship between abstraction and representation. *Journal for Research in Mathematics Education, 33*(1), 30–45.

Keefe, J. W. (1987). *Learning style: Theory and practice.* Reston, VA: National Association of Secondary School Principals.

Kluger, J., & Park, A. (2001, April 30). The quest for a superkid. *Time*, 50–55.

Knowles, T., & Brown, D. F. (2000). What every middle school teacher should know. Westerville, OH: National Middle School Association.

Kolb, D. A. (1984). *Experiential learning: Experience as the source of learning and development*. Englewood Cliffs, NJ: Princeton-Hall.

Kounin, J. (1977). *Discipline and group management in classrooms*. New York: Holt, Rinehart,and Winston.

Krug, S. E. (1993). Leadership craft and the crafting of school leaders. *Phi Delta Kappan, 75*(3), 240–244.

Lapsley, D. K. (1993). Toward an integrated theory of adolescent ego development: The "new look" at adolescent egocentrism. *American Journal of Orthopsychiatry, 63,* 562–571.

Los Angeles County Schools (2003). Los Angeles County Schools Homepage. Retrieved November 26, 2003, from http://www.lacoe.edu/orgs/125/index.cfm

Lybarger, M. B. (1991). The historiography of social studies: Retrospect, circumspect, and prospect. In J. P. Shaver (Ed.), *Handbook of research on social studies teaching and learning* (pp. 3–15). New York: MacMillan.

Lyons, A. A., & Pinnell, G. S. (2001). *Systems for change in literacy education: A guide to professional development*. Portsmouth, NH: Heinemann.

Marsh, C. J., & Willis, G. (2003). *Curriculum: Alternative approaches, ongoing issues* (3rd ed.). Upper Saddle River, NJ: Merrill.

Maryland State Department of Education.(2003). *Administrative "look fors"* Retrieved November 25, 2003, from Maryland State Department of Education Web site: http://www.msde.state.md.us/hsimprovement/adminstratorlookfors.html

Maxwell, R. J., & Meiser, M. J. (2001). *Teaching English in the middle and secondary schools* (3rd ed.). Upper Saddle River, NJ: Merrill.

McBride, M., & Skau, K. G. (1995). Trust, empowerment, and reflection: Essentials of supervision. *Journal of Curriculum and Supervision, 10*(3), 262–277.

McGee, L. M., Charlesworth, R., Check, M., & Check, E. (1982). Metalinguistic knowledge: Another look at beginning reading. *Childhood Education, 59*(1), 123–127.

McGreal, T. (1983). *Effective teacher evaluation*. Alexandria, VA: Association for Supervision and Curriculum.

McMillan, J. H. (2000). Fundamental assessment principles for teachers and school administrators. *Practical Assessment, Research & Evaluation, 7*(8). Retrieved January 5, 2004, from http://PAREonline.net/getvn.asp?v=7&n=8

McNeil, J. D. (1990). Curriculum: A comprehensive introduction (4th ed.). Glenview, IL: Scott, Foresman/Little, Brown Higher Education.

McTighe, J., & Lyman, F. T. (1988). Cueing thinking in the classroom: The promise of theory-embedded tools. *Educational Leadership, 45*(7), 18–24.

Mendelson, B. K., White, D. R., & Mendelson, M. J. (1996). Self-esteem and body esteem: Effects of gender, age, and weight. *Journal of Applied Developmental Psychology, 17*(3), 321–346.

Mizell, H. (1994, July). *Focusing the middle school: The principal's role.* Remarks made at The Middle School Principals Institute at Jefferson County Schools. Louisville, Kentucky. Retrieved November 2, 2003, from http://www. middleweb.com/Newprincipal.html

Mohr, L. C. (1999). 20 Ways to Foster Creativity in Your Students. *ENC Focus* 6(2), 36–37. Retrieved December 21, 2003, from Eisenhower National Clearinghouse: www.enc.org

Munson, B. (1998). Peers observing peers: The better way to observe teachers. *Contemporary Education, 69*(2), 108–111.

Murphy, S. M. (1997). Designing portfolio assessment: Programs to enhance learning. *The Clearing House, 71*(2), 81–84.

National Center for Education Statistics (1996). *Are high school teachers teaching core subjects without college majors or minors those subjects?* (NCES Publication No. 96–839). Washington, DC: U.S. Government Printing Office.

National Commission on Social Studies in Schools. (1989). *Charting a course: Social studies for the 21st Century.* Washington, DC: National Council for the Social Studies.

National Council for the Social Studies (1997*). National standards for social studies teachers.* Silver Spring, MD: National Council for the Social Studies.

National Council of Teachers of English and International Reading Association (1996). *Standards for the English language arts.* Urbana, IL: National Council of Teachers of English and Newark, DE: International Reading Association.

National Council of Teachers of Mathematics. (2000a). *Standards for school mathematics.* Reston, VA: National Council of Teachers of Mathematics.

National Council of Teachers of Mathematics (2000b). *Principles and standards for school mathematics.* Retrieved October 31, 2003, from http://standards.nctm. org/document

National Partnership for Excellence and Accountability in Teaching. (1999). *Revisioning Professional Development: What Learner-Centered Professional Development Looks Like.* Retrieved March 10, 2003, from http://www.nsdc. org/NPEAT213.pdf

National Research Council (1996). *National science education standards.* Washington, DC: National Academy Press. Retrieved January 4, 2004, from www.nsta.org/standards

National Science Board. (2002). *Science and engineering indicators 2002.* Arlington, VA: National Science Foundation, Retrieved December 13, 2003, from www.nsf.gov/seb/srs/seind02/pdf

National Science Education Standards. (1996). *National science education standards.* Washington, DC: National Academy Press, Author. Retrieved January 4, 2004, from www.nsta.org/standards

Newmann, F. M., & Wehlage, G. G. (1993). Standards of authentic instruction. Educational Leadership, 50(7), 8–12.

Ogden, L. (1998). A better way to supervise. *Thrust for Educational Leadership, 8(5),* 20–22.

O'Neil, J. (1998). Constructivism—wanted: Deep understanding. In J. O'Neil & S. Willis (Eds.), *Transforming classroom practice* (pp. 49–70). Alexandria, VA: Association for Supervision and Curriculum Development.

Ormrod, J. E. (2000). *Educational psychology: Developing learners* (3rd ed.). Upper Saddle River, NJ: Merrill.

Panasonic Foundation (n.d.). About essential school system purpose and responsibilities: A Panasonic Foundation protocol. Retrieved July 22, 2003, from http://www.panasonic.com/MECA/foundation/esspar.html

Pajak, E. (1993). *Approaches to clinical supervision: Alternatives for improving instruction.* Norwood, MA: Christopher-Gordon Publishers.

Parkay, F. W., & Hass, G. (2000). *Curriculum planning: A contemporary approach* (7th ed.). Needham Heights, MA: Allyn & Bacon.

Pejza, J. P. (1994, April). *Lead, follow, or get out of the way: Transformational leadership.* A paper prepared for the annual meeting of the National Catholic Educational Association: Anaheim, CA. (ERIC Document Reproduction Service No. ED375496)

Piaget, J. (1952). *The origins of intelligence in children.* (M. Cook, Trans.). New York: Norton.

Piaget, J. (1969). *The child's perception of time.* (A. J. Pomerans, Trans.). New York: Basic Books.

Piaget, J. (1977). *The development of thought: Elaboration of cognitive structures.* New York: Viking.

Poplin, M. S. (1992). The leader's new role: Looking to the growth of teachers. *Educational Leadership, 49*(4), 10–11.

Ramey, C. T., & Ramey, S. L. (1996, February). *At risk does not mean doomed.* Paper presented at the annual meeting of the American Association of Science.

Reys, R. E., Lindquist, M. M., Lambdin, D. V., Smith, N. L., & Suydam, M. N. (2004). *Helping children learn mathematics* (7th ed.). Hoboken, NJ: Wiley.

Rodgers, J. L. (1996). Sexual transitions in adolescence. In J. A. Graber, J. Brooks Gunn, & A. C. Peterson (Eds.), *Transitions through adolescence: Interpersonal domains and context* (pp. 85–110). Mahwah, NJ: Erlbaum.

Ross, R., & Kurtz, R. (1993). Making manipulatives work: A strategy for success. *Arithmetic Teacher, 40,* 254–257.

Sanborn, J., & Sanborn, E. (1994). A conversation on portfolios. *Middle School Journal, 26*(1), 26–29.

Savage, T. V., & Armstrong, D. G. (1996). *Effective teaching in elementary social studies* (3rd ed.). Englewood Cliffs, NJ: Merrill.

Selman, R. L. (1976). Social-cognitive understanding: A guide to educational and clinical practice. In T. Lickona (Ed.), *Moral development and behavior: Theory, research, and social issues* (pp. 299–316). New York: Holt, Rinehart, & Winston.

Seventh-day Adventist North American Division Office of Education. (2002). Socratic seminar observation form. Retrieved November 29, 2003, from http://curriculumfutures.org/assessment/a05-01f.html

Sharan, S., & Sharan, Y. (1976). *Small-group teaching.* Englewood Cliffs, NJ: Educational Technology Publications.

Short, K. G., & Pierce, K. M. (Eds.). (1990). *Talking about books; Creating literate communities.* Portsmouth, NH: Heinemann.

Silver, H. F., & Hanson, J. R. (1998). *Learning styles and strategies* (3rd ed.). Woodbridge, NJ: The Thoughtful Education Press.

Silver, H. F., Strong, R. W., & Perini, M. J. (1997). Integrating learning styles and multiple intelligences. *Educational Leadership, 55*(1), 22–27.

Silver, H. F., Strong, R. W., & Perini, M. J. (2000). *So each may learn: Integrating learning styles and multiple intelligences.* Alexandria, VA: Association for Supervision and Curriculum Development.

Simmons, R. G., & Blythe, D. A. (1987). *Moving into adolescence: The impact of pubertal change and school context.* Hawthorne, NY: Aldine de Gruyter.

Skretta, J., & Fisher, V. (2002). The walk-through crew. *Principal Leadership, 3*(3). Retrieved October 5, 2003, from http://www.principals.org/news/pl_walkthrgh_1102.cfm

Smith, F. (1978). *Psycholinguistics and reading.* New York: Holt, Rinehart, & Winston.

Smylie, M., & Conyers, J. (1991). Changing conceptions of teaching influence the future of staff development. *Journal of Staff Development, 12*(1), 11–17.

Sowell, E. J. (1989). Effects of manipulative materials in mathematics instruction. *Journal for Research in Mathematics Education. 20*(5), 498–505.

Sowell, E. J. (1996). *Curriculum an integrative introduction.* Englewood Cliffs, NJ: Prentice-Hall.

Sowell, E. R., Delis, D., Stiles, J., & Jernigan, T. L. (2001). Improved memory functioning and frontal lobe maturation between childhood and adolescence: A structural MRI study. *Journal of the International Neuropsychological Society, 7*(3), 312–322.

Spodek, B., & Sracho, O. N. (1994). *Right from the start: Teaching children ages three to eight.* Boston: Allyn & Bacon.

Sprenger, M. (1999). *Learning and memory: The brain in action.* Alexandria, VA: Association for Supervision and Curriculum Development.

Stahl, S. (1999). Different strokes for different folks: A critique of learning styles. *American Federation of Teachers,* 27–31.

Standards for the English Language Arts (1996). *Standards for the English language arts.* Urbana, IL: National Council of Teachers of English and Newark, DE: International Reading Association.

Steinberg, L. (1996). *Beyond the classroom: Why school reform has failed and what parents need to do.* New York: Simon & Schuster.

Stern, B. S. (2002). *Social studies: Standards meaning and understanding.* Larchmont, NY: Eye On Education.

Stiggins, R. J. (1994). *Student-centered classroom assessment.* NY: Macmillan.

Stone, R. (2002). *Best practices for high school classrooms: What award-winning secondary teachers do.* Thousand Oaks, CA: Corwin Press.

Strebe, J. D. (1996). The collaborative classroom. In R. L. Canady & M. D. Rettig (Eds.), *Teaching in the block: Strategies for engaging active learners* (pp. 65–106). Larchmont, NY: Eye On Education.

Suchman, J. R. (1962). *The elementary school training program in scientific inquiry* (Report No. NDEA-VIIA-216). Urbana, IL: University of Illinois. (ERIC Document Reproduction Service No. ED003530)

Sullivan, S., & Glanz, J. (2000). Alternative approaches to supervision: Cases from the field. *Journal of Curriculum and Supervision, 15*(3), 212–235.

Sylwester, R. (1995). *A celebration of neurons: An educator's guide to the human brain.* Alexandria, VA: Association for Supervision and Curriculum Development.

Thorton, S. J. (1991). Teacher as curricular-instructional gatekeeper in social studies. In J. P. Shaver (Ed.), *Handbook of research on social studies teaching and learning* (pp. 237–248). New York: MacMillan.

Tomlinson, C. A. (1999). *The differentiated classroom: Responding to the needs of all learners.* Alexandria, VA: Association for Supervision and Curriculum Development.

Tomlinson, C. A. (2001). Standards and the art of teaching: Crafting high-quality classrooms. *NASSP Bulletin, 85*(622), 107–114.

Tomlinson, C. A., & Allan, S. D. (2000). *Leadership for differentiating schools and classrooms.* Alexandria, VA: Association for Supervision and Curriculum Development.

United States Department of Education (2002). Why *No child left behind* is important to America. Retrieved November 25, 2003, http://www.ed.gov/nclb/overview/importance/edlite-index.html

Walker, D. E. (1998). *Strategies for teaching differently: On the block or not.* Thousand Oaks, CA: Corwin.

Wesson, K. (2002). Creating learning environments that are "brain considerate" and "enriched." Retrieved November 7, 2003, from Sciencemaster Web site: http://www.sciencemaster.com/wesson/pdfs/enriched_learning.pdf

Willerman, M., McNeely, S. L., & Koffman, E. C. (1991*). Teachers helping teachers: Peer observation and assistance.* New York: Praeger.

Williams, V. (Ed.) (1998). *Conceptual and practical issues in school leadership: Insights and innovations from the U.S. and abroad.* San Francisco: Jossey Bass.

Wilson, B., & Cole, P. (1991). A review of cognitive teaching models. *Educational Technology Research and Development, 39*(4), 47–64.

Winebrenner, S. (1992). *Teaching gifted kids in the regular classroom: Strategies and techniques every teacher can use to meet the academic needs of the gifted and talented.* Minneapolis, MN: Free Spirit.

Wolfe, P. (2001). *Brain matters: Translating research into classroom practice.* Alexandria, VA: Association for Supervision and Curriculum Development.

Wolfe, P. & Brandt, R. (1998). What do we know from brain research? *Educational Leadership, 56*(3), 8–13.

Wolk, R. A. (2003). Trivial pursuits. *Teacher Magazine, 14*(04), 4. Retrieved December 14, 2002, from http://www.teachermagazine.org/tmstory.cfm?slug=04persp.h14

Woolfolk, A. E. (1998). *Educational psychology* (7th ed.). Boston: Allyn & Bacon.

Yerrick, R. (1998). Reconstructing classroom facts: Transforming lower-track science classrooms. *Journal of Science Teacher Education, 9*(2), 241–270.

Zarrillo, J. (1989). Teacher's interpretations of literature-based reading. *Reading Teacher, 43*(1), 22–28.

Zepeda, S. J. (1997, September). *Self-analysis of teaching.* Workshop for the Norman School District New Teacher Forum. Norman, OK.

Zepeda, S. J. (2002). Linking portfolio development to clinical supervision: A case study. *The Journal of Curriculum and Supervision, 18*(1), 83–102.

Zepeda, S. J. (2003a). *Instructional supervision: Applying tools and concepts.* Larchmont, NY: Eye On Education.

Zepeda, S. J. (2003b). *The principal as instructional leader: A handbook for supervisors.* Larchmont, NY: Eye On Education.

Zepeda, S. J. (2004). *Instructional leadership for school improvement.* Larchmont, NY: Eye On Education.

Zepeda, S. J., & Mayers, R. S. (2000). *Supervision and staff development in the block.* Larchmont, NY: Eye On Education.